Better Homes and Gardens®

garden rooms

Better Homes and Gardens® Books
Des Moines, Iowa

Better Homes and Gardens® Books
An imprint of Meredith® Books

Garden Rooms
Writer: Julie Martens
Editor and Project Manager: Kate Carter Frederick
Art Director: Lyne Neymeyer
Project Coordinator: Beth Ann Edwards
Photo Coordinator: Lois Sutherland
Copy Chief: Terri Fredrickson
Copy and Production Editor: Victoria Forlini
Editorial Operations Manager: Karen Schirm
Managers, Book Production: Pam Kvitne, Marjorie J. Schenkelberg
Contributing Copy Editor: Sharon McHaney
Contributing Proofreaders: Chardel Blaine, Elsa Kramer, Alison Glascock
Contributing Technical Editor: David Haupert
Illustrators: Roxanne LeMoine, Tom Rosborough
Indexer: Deborah L. Baier
Inputters: Janet Anderson, Connie Webb
Electronic Production Coordinator: Paula Forest
Editorial and Design Assistants: Mary Lee Gavin, Karen McFadden, Kathy Stevens

Meredith® Books
Publisher and Editor in Chief: James D. Blume
Design Director: Matt Strelecki
Managing Editor: Gregory H. Kayko
Executive Editor, Home Improvement and Gardening: Benjamin W. Allen
Executive Editor, Gardening: Michael McKinley

Director, Operations: George A. Susral
Director, Production: Douglas M. Johnston

Vice President and General Manager: Douglas J. Guendel

Better Homes and Gardens® Magazine
Editor in Chief: Karol DeWulf Nickell
Deputy Editor, Gardens and Outdoor Living: Mark Kane

Meredith Publishing Group
President, Publishing Group: Stephen M. Lacy
Vice President-Publishing Director: Bob Mate

Meredith Corporation
Chairman and Chief Executive Officer: William T. Kerr

Chairman of the Executive Committee: E. T. Meredith III

Cover photograph: Richard Felber

All of us at Better Homes and Gardens® Books are dedicated to providing you with information and ideas to enhance your home and garden. We welcome your comments and suggestions. Write to us at: Better Homes and Gardens Books, Garden Editorial Department, 1716 Locust St., Des Moines, IA 50309-3023.

If you would like to purchase any of our gardening, cooking, crafts, home improvement, or home decorating and design books, check wherever quality books are sold. Or visit us at bhgbooks.com

garden
rooms

introduction

a sense of place

Imagine a house with no walls: neither exterior walls for privacy, nor interior walls to separate one room from another, just open, undefined space. Few of us would want to live in such a setting. To make a house a home, the place needs a family of rooms, each with a specially designated role.

Landscapes are much the same. The best ones provide private, shady hideaways as well as open areas for entertaining. They balance a blend of expansive spaces and views with cloistered retreats for rest, reflection, and rejuvenation. They offer rooms for dining, for sleeping, for reading, and even for bathing. Their decorative elements help create a sense of place that insulates you from the world yet somehow connects you to it. That's the beauty of a garden room. It unites you with the natural surroundings that are easily overlooked in this age of glowing computer and television screens and artificially created environments.

A sense of place provides one of the strongest influences on garden design today, resulting in garden rooms that reflect where and how you live. Let your region's climate and environment guide and distinguish your garden plans.

building blocks
right: **The basics of a garden room (floor, walls, and furnishings) flow together to form a destination that's cozy and comfortable.**

in the beginning

Garden rooms hark back to biblical times and the exotic hanging gardens of Babylon. Through the ages, garden rooms donned a formal look that eventually graced the sumptuous homes of European aristocracy. But these rooms served to please the eyes more than the soul.

Today's garden rooms create places we desire to be, not just places to see. They form nooks and niches in the garden where we curl our toes in the grass, sip our morning coffee with the newspaper in hand, and play board games with our children. They remind us of favorite vacation destinations, soothe us with their sense of sanctuary, and extend our indoor living spaces. Garden rooms are all about expanding our comfort zone. They help us relax after a busy day, provide a place for friends and family to gather, and charm us with the promise of reconnecting with nature.

pavilion splendor

above: Crowned in fragrant roses and surrounded by hollyhocks, columbines, and a host of lush perennials, this pavilion frames a spot for quiet reflection. The structure also inspires outdoor entertaining in a comfort-packed setting. When the sun sets, candlelit lanterns help create a festive mood.

inside out

left: When planning garden rooms, position them so that your home's windows and doors look out on the beautiful scenery year-round. Wonderful vistas of beautiful outdoor living spaces entice you to come out and play.

introduction

expand your borders

Garden rooms extend living areas beyond the walls of a house, spilling the stuff of everyday indoor life into the surrounding green space. With the price of land continuing to skyrocket and the size of lots shrinking, a yard counts as premium living space. If you have a yard, why not transform it into a place you yearn to be, to sit, work, eat, sleep, interact, and find solitude?

Create a room in your garden or divide your yard into a series of rooms that fulfill all these needs and more. The process is easy. Begin by choosing a place that lends itself to transformation. Add boundaries (shrubs, fences, walls) and you'll achieve a sheltered, private room outdoors.

overhead artistry

above: A ceiling defines a room with ease. An umbrella covers this dining area, transforming it into a shaded room.

woodland ramblings

right: A garden folly captures the imagination as a secluded destination. Furnishings expand the folly's usefulness.

walls to rooms

Whereas walls and fences provide privacy, trees, hedges, and bermed flower beds offer a living framework for a room. Structures, such as a gazebo, an arbor, or a pergola, define a garden room instantly. A sense of enclosure separates the place from surrounding spaces and enhances its character.

Begin the process of embellishing your garden room by answering these questions: Do you enjoy dining outdoors? Do you need a shady, secluded spot for relaxing after work? Do you want a resort-style room, complete with a spa? Do your children or pets require room to play? Include everyone in your household when you prioritize needs and desires, then plan accordingly.

something from nothing

above left: A garden swing, enclosed with an arbor, provides a garden hideaway for engaging conversation or quiet contemplation. Lattice and a backdrop of shrubs bolster the level of privacy.

restful retreat

left: In open spaces, a wall added as background to a seating area clearly defines a room's boundaries. Depending on the effect you want, open windows allow breezes to move freely through the room, whereas windowpanes shelter the area.

introduction

tie it all together

Just like a floor plan for a home, a garden design ideally flows together, and the rooms have logical locations. For instance, place a children's play area so it's visible from a deck or patio, but far enough away to prevent a ball from breaking a window. Site a sunny perennial border so its flowers grace an indoor breakfast nook with festive color. Situate a potting area nearby to keep gardening tools, soil amendments, watering cans, and buckets handy.

Connect rooms with meandering paths and mark entrances with a stylish arbor, a change in surface underfoot, or a door. Count on hardscape, or the portion of a landscape that is not green and growing, to delineate separate areas of the garden. Hardscape elements include paths, steps, edging, patios, and decks.

Soften the hardscape with plants and accessories that express your personality and suit your lifestyle. Over time, you'll create a space that ministers to body and soul.

Use fabrics freely, selecting weather-resistant blends developed for outdoor use. Include several pieces of comfortable furniture, night lighting, and a water feature. Add vacation-style amenities, such as a spa and outdoor stereo speakers so that time spent in your backyard turns every day into a holiday.

using this book

Explore the array of garden rooms on the following pages and find inspiration for your outdoor space.

alfresco fare
right: An elegant iron table and chairs, situated under the canopy of a stately tree, transform a bare spot into a lovely outdoor dining area.

Throughout this book, you'll discover projects designed to transform ordinary areas into inviting, comfortable rooms. The projects include materials lists and a quick-glance summary of the time and skill required to complete them.

You'll also find a cost guide, indicated by dollar signs. A "$" indicates that the project can be built for $50 or less. A "$$" depicts projects costing $51–$100. Projects costing more than $100 are indicated with "$$$."

Follow our plans step by step or use them as a launchpad to invent your own projects. Nothing stands between you and the garden rooms of your dreams. Get ready to create your garden escape.

From quick fixes to full-blown landscaping projects, find the gardening solutions you need at **www.bhg.com/ bkgardening solutions**

wired for enjoyment
above: For memorable outdoor meals, set a table that's ripe with garden delights, featuring fresh flowers and floral-theme servingware. Serve dishes brimming with garden edibles.

finishing touches
left: Complete a room with decorative trims, using what you have on hand. Transform a cast-off watering can into a vase for dried flowers by sprucing it up with acrylic paints.

the
basics

from start to finish

To build the house of your dreams, begin with a plan that's a no-frills sketch of boundaries: walls, floors, ceilings, and doors. Then pencil in spaces, setting aside rooms for gathering, playing, resting, and relaxing. One by one, you add the elements that craft your home sweet home, making something livable from open space. The process is the same in the garden.

choose your direction Before you break ground on your garden room, take inventory. Ask yourself simple questions guaranteed to give you solid direction in creating an outside chockfull of living spaces: What do you want to do in your garden? Will you entertain guests, have family picnics, or gather around a fire pit? Does the idea of an outdoor study beckon? Do you need a play area for children or a place for pets to run? Do you wish to grow vegetables or flowers or perhaps a Provençal blend of both? Do you seek a restful retreat complete with a spa or a small water feature? As you answer these and other questions, you'll discover the types of rooms you'll want to complement your lifestyle.

define the rooms Divide and conquer your yard using the same space-partitioning techniques that transform the open expanse of your indoor living area into rooms: floors, walls, halls, and structures. In the garden, flooring sprawls underfoot in myriad ways, from a lush carpet of lawn to hardwood decking or easy-care concrete, flagstone, or pavers. Walls take form with lattice, hedges, fences, and stucco or stone.

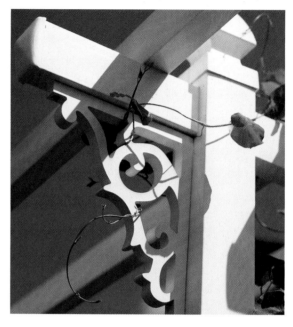

Paths serve as hallways, connecting outdoor rooms and directing traffic. Structures add focal points, shelter, storage, and more.

finishing touches Outdoors, plants and garden embellishments enhance a room by softening the more industrious hardscape elements. Carefully combined plants and decorative items create an everyday getaway with the look and feel of another culture or region. Imagine the tropics or a Mexican-style courtyard outside your back door.

Count on greenery (trees, shrubs, or flowers) to fill many roles in the garden: screening a view here, enclosing a bench there, and adding living color everywhere. Decorative touches, such as artwork, candles, or a collage of favorite collectibles, reveal your personality and complete the scene.

planning & designing

dreams come true

Cultivate a personal vision for your garden room. Begin by surveying your yard and putting what you see onto paper. Use accurate measurements to draw the existing features of your lot (house, patio or deck, planting beds, trees, shrubs, walkways, and such) to scale. Lay tracing paper over the map and indicate site characteristics, such as sunlight, soil type, and wind exposure, to help you figure out plant choices later.

stencil artistry

above: Armed with colored pencils and a garden template, embellish a bird's-eye-view drawing of your yard with the components of your dreamscape by stenciling in plants, walkways, fencing, and more into the layout.

expert advice

right: Brainstorm ideas with a landscape designer, crafting a personalized yard plan to fit a specific budget and time frame. If you wish, ask the designer to supervise the construction phase of your landscape.

Match the dream components of your outdoor rooms to the natural attributes of your yard, such as a reflecting pond for an empty courtyard or entryway, or a family picnic and croquet area on an expanse of shaded lawn. On another piece of tracing paper, pencil in the rooms you'd like to add to your yard. Indicate access points and traffic flow patterns. Mentally walk through the areas, considering the interconnectedness of each room. Continually ask yourself if each room's placement and flow enhance outdoor living or if it makes simple tasks, such as harvesting fresh herbs for dinner, a major expedition. Last, use a fresh paper overlay to draw the details (structures, plants, and decor) that personalize your plan. From this point, implement your plan or meet with a professional to garner help in bringing your sketch to life.

inch by inch

above: **If you must work alone and need to anchor a tape measure to mark a straight line, slip a large nail through the end of the tape and into the ground.**

planning & designing checklist

- Couple your design with a plan of action that includes a time frame. Stretch projects over time to keep costs down. Do the work yourself whenever possible to save money and increase your personal-pride investment in the yard.

- Compare prices. If any part of your project requires a contractor, secure itemized bids from at least two contractors and compare them line by line.

- Ask for a written guarantee of any contractor's work. Ask for proof of their liability insurance. Set start and finish dates for each project.

- Rescue and reuse materials from your current yard before you begin a remodel. Transplant shrubs and perennials into holding beds and then move hardscape pieces. Recycle chunks of an old concrete walk into a stacked retaining wall or stepping-stones.

- Think ahead when laying electrical or water lines. Include extra outlets and spigots to accommodate future yard improvements in areas that remain undeveloped.

- Always invest in soil amendments for planting beds. Add organic material (compost, rotted manure, and chopped leaves) by the truckload before you tuck the first plant into a bed. Great soil grows great plants.

site preparation

survey your area

First assess the lay of your land, focusing on the pros and cons of your landscape. Note everything, from areas of shade to wind exposure, from a good sunset view to eyesores, or wet areas where water collects. Note these aspects on the basic map you made of your yard (see page 16). Stand inside your home and gaze out the windows. What you do to your yard will affect the view from indoors. Make a list of the views you presently savor, along with ones you'd like to change.

Before you construct anything, have a firm understanding of local building codes, easements, and neighborhood covenants that may affect your property. Contact utility companies to determine the location of underground lines. Be present when a utilities worker marks the lines; make sure all labels are clear. Add these lines to your yard map.

drafter's delight

above: Use graph paper to draw your landscape to scale. Be sure to include underground utility lines on your sketch.

plant tapestry

right: Before planting, set perennials and shrubs still in their nursery pots into place on the prepared bed. Shift pots as necessary to create an artful arrangement and to accommodate spacing for mature plant size.

Survey your yard through the seasons and marry problem areas with solutions that match your garden room wish list. Does the western sun beat mercilessly on your family room all summer? Insulate your home with shade-casting fruit trees that dish up garden-fresh fare for your family. Do spring rains create a seasonal swamp in your backyard? Address that soggy space with a water feature or moisture-loving plants.

geometry works

above: Symmetrical beds add a formal element to a suburban backyard. Use a structural feature, such as a tuteur (*shown*), a fountain, or an oversized container, to play center stage in your backyard scene.

side-yard switch

left: Transform an ugly-duckling side yard of grass into a graceful-as-a-swan allée (a tree-lined walkway). Begin by removing turf; then set balled and burlapped trees into place. Choose trees that will grow more up than out, such as colonnade apple trees, narrow upright junipers, or columnar hornbeams. Mark one entry to your allée with an arch; place a bench at the other end.

hardscaping: building a wall

cost	make it	skill
$$$	2-3 weekends	moderate

you will need

- stone
- stakes
- string
- level
- shovel
- gravel
- sledgehammer
- trowel
- chisel

stack 'em up

There's something timeless and enchanting about a stone wall. Whether it frames a garden room or a planting area, a stone wall boasts a rugged look that suits most gardens and adds a sense of permanence.

When planning a wall, consider its size, shape, and purpose. Enclosed by a wall, garden rooms gain privacy, wind protection, and an attractive backdrop. A walled planting area, on the other hand, rises above ground level to define a room without blocking the view. A retaining wall refutes the claim of gravity on a hill, transforming unused sloping ground into terraced planting space. A knee-high wall proves moderately easy to build.

Learn about the types of building materials available in your area by visiting a landscaping retailer, building center, or stone yard. Bring along measurements and ask the staff to help you determine which types of stone or other materials suit your needs and budget. Flat stone makes the process easier; use interlocking stones (or modular masonry blocks) if you prefer. Save money by choosing a plentiful native stone or by building with techniques featuring concrete block, straw bale, or adobe.

enduringly yours

right: **A stacked-stone wall adds texture and scale to a garden. Flat, rectangular stone produces a tight fit and a sturdy wall.**

1 groundwork To build a dry-stack stone wall, purchase stone and underlayment (gravel) and arrange a delivery. Minimize hauling by having stone piled close to your work site. Lift with your legs and not with your back to avoid injury. Use stakes and string to mark the wall's course. Pull the string taut between the stakes, making sure it's level. Dig a shallow trench that's just below the frost line in your region; local building authorities can give you that measurement.

2 well grounded If you're working on a slope, cut the back side of the trench at an angle slanting into the slope. For drainage, line the trench with about an inch of gravel. Place the longest stones on the bottom layer. The fewer the joints in the first layer, the less chance of freeze-thaw cycles heaving your wall. Level stones as you lay them; tap stones with the handle end of a sledgehammer to settle them into place. Trowel soil beneath a wobbly stone to stabilize it. If you must cut a stone, use a sledgehammer, and chisel.

3 stone upon stone Stack stones so that each stone bridges a joint in the row below it. If you're building a retaining wall on a slope, dig a hole into the slope every 4 to 6 feet and lay a long stone perpendicular to the wall, with one end resting on the wall and the rest of the stone extending into the hole. Use these same techniques whether you're building a straight or a curved wall. (Check local building codes and consider hiring a contractor to build a wall more than 3 feet tall.)

hardscaping: laying a floor

cost	make it	skill
$$-$$$	weekend	easy

you will need

- spray paint or flour
- spade
- road-grade gravel
- hand tamper or plate compactor
- builder's sand
- rake
- pavers
- diamond or wet saw
- rubber mallet
- broom

floored!

When considering a floor for a garden room, think beyond lawn. Although turf blends into any outdoor scene, hard surfaces offer decorative panache and durability.

Choose flooring for your garden rooms and the paths that connect them knowing that the surface must endure more than foot traffic and the vagaries of weather. Hardscape must also support heavy objects or items that require a level, solid surface, such as furniture, a grill, or a spa.

Use similar flooring materials throughout your garden to link diverse areas or rooms with a common design theme. Concrete, brick, and stone provide sturdy surfaces that last a lifetime. Brick pavers come in a variety of sizes, colors, and shapes that are easily adaptable to patios or paths. From cobbles to stepping-stone-size pavers, bricks offer design possibilities that conquer curves with ease and shape edging as well. Rent a diamond or wet saw to cut bricks.

wall-to-wall bricks

right: Roll out your own garden-variety red carpet with red bricks. These kiln-fired pavers offer endless pattern variations and longtime persistence, bearing up well through seasonal extremes.

1 set the course To construct a brick floor, such as this path that wraps around a wall, mark the floor's boundaries with spray paint or flour; then remove the sod. Use a spade to excavate the soil to a depth of 5 inches plus the thickness of your flooring material. Spread a 4-inch layer of road-grade gravel in the trench; tamp it down. For floors less than 80 square feet, compact the gravel using a hand tamper. For larger floors, rent a plate compactor.

2 complete the floor Build the wall (see page 21) then complete the floor. Add an inch of builder's sand to the floor, leveling it with the back of a rake. Set pavers on top of the sand, snugly against one another, in the desired pattern. Use a rubber mallet to tamp pavers into place. Spread a ½-inch layer of dry sand over the floor. Sweep it into the cracks between the pavers, then water the floor using a fine spray. If the floor feels wobbly over time, sweep in more sand.

stone smorgasbord

Crushed rock comes in many types and builds a floor that drains well and requires little maintenance other than occasional raking and replenishing. Visit a stone yard, quarry, or landscaping retailer to discover the range of alternatives. In general, a ton of crushed rock covers 90 to 100 square feet. Delivered from the quarry, crushed rock outbargains bagged rock mulch. Avoid loose stone as a floor treatment in areas frequented by rolling carts, high heels, or chairs that require movement, such as those around a dining table.

adding structures

structurally sound

Count on garden
structures to frame
spaces in your yard,
creating sensible,
tasteful subdivisions
of the landscape. As
focal points, structures
punctuate a garden.
Some structures
provide overhead
shelter, offering a dry
place on a rainy day
and a refreshing pool
of shade on sweltering
afternoons. Other
structures define
boundaries for your
garden rooms and
transform unused
areas into your favorite
gathering places.

aspire higher

right: **A corner trellis
and storage benches
add interest to an
ordinary deck. The
substantial posts,
overhead lattice, and
potted plants create
a sense of sitting in a
private, lushly planted
garden. The bonuses:
cushions, storage
areas, and plenty
of natural lighting.**

garden structure glossary

arbor: Arches or latticework; for vertical interest, supporting vines, and providing shade. Types of arbors reflect architectural styles, such as Arts and Crafts or modern.

folly: A garden house designed to offer protection from weather and scenic interest; originated in English estate gardens.

gazebo: An open, airy place that provides shelter and a view of the garden.

pergola: An open roof supported by columns or posts, covering a room or a walkway. Vines typically scramble a across pergola roof.

ramada: The Spanish word for arbor. Open-sided and sometimes attached to a building, a ramada has a solid roof (wood shingles, tile, or such).

trellis: This two-dimensional structure helps support and train climbing or vining plants and add vertical interest to the garden.

Find inspiration for structural elements in classic architectural design motifs, famous historic gardens, and magazines. Keep a clipping file of ideas, making notes as you mentally translate them to suit the scale and style of your home.

Although the price of structural elements varies widely, prefabricated structures may cost more than ones you build yourself. Designing your own structure and hiring a professional to tackle construction are other options. Whatever method you choose, don't skimp on materials. Top-quality components cost more but last longer.

Before placing any structure in your garden, stand inside your home and visualize the feature in place. Make sure you'll enjoy the view from indoors as well as from various areas of the yard.

salvage style
above left: **A garden folly mirrors a classic icon of Greco-Roman architecture: the rotunda. This retreat features an upended satellite-dish roof and beachcombed wharf piling posts.**

walk this way
left: **Arbored walkways lead you along a wooded path and provide resting spots. Fenced for safety on steep terrain, the arbors add structural interest.**

adding plants

make room for greenery

Landscaping pays. Using plants to improve the aesthetics of your property increases its value. Properly positioned plants also reduce home heating and cooling costs.

But plants do more than put money in your pocket. They beautifully soften a scene and frame its outstanding features. Imagine the view in this cozy corner (*right*) without plants. Bricks and concrete would steal the show in a room that lacks definition and invitation. Add plants, and voilà! Hedges form walls that enhance privacy. Trimmed boxwood borders artfully echo the room's angular design. Colorful annuals delight the eye.

Include plants in your landscape plan (see page 16), indicating existing and new plantings, but wait to sink a trowel into soil until you have installed structures, walkways, irrigation lines, lighting, and such. Place hardscape first to avoid damaging plant roots with heavy equipment and digging. Stay away from existing trees and shrubs when using heavy machinery to avoid compacting the soil and injuring roots or stems. Avoid excavating deeply around trees.

Prepare planting beds according to the soil needs of the flowers and shrubs you'll be adding. Your local extension service provides soil tests and suggests ways to address soil deficiencies. When planting, place the largest plants first. Imagine plants at their mature size and give them room to grow. Tight quarters require compact plants; choose dwarf varieties with smaller potential than their standard-size cousins.

top to bottom

right: Mimic nature in your approach to landscaping by planting layers: trees overhead, shrubs from waist- to headhigh, and groundcovers underfoot. Fill the spaces in between with perennials and annuals.

Plan ahead for your plants' maintenance requirements too. If you don't have lots of time to tend the garden, choose native plants for easy-care beauty. Select drought-resistant, disease-resistant, and slow-growing varieties. Although annuals offer stunning, season-long color, they also require annual replacement, as their name suggests. If you garden where winter brings snow cover, include plants that stitch interest into a white-quilted landscape.

ideal plant deals

Make the most of your plant budget by following a few simple plant purchasing tricks:

- Shop with a list. Avoid impulse buying. Stick to your plan.

- Plan to plant in spring and fall. Find the best selection, especially of perennials, early in the season. As spring turns to summer, look for bargains at seasonal garden centers, such as those at grocery stores.

- Predetermine which size of pot you want and shop for plants on that basis. If you're planting a tree for shade, for example, start with the largest one your budget allows and enjoy the tree's shade in your lifetime. Buy perennials in the largest pots affordable for a more finished-looking garden. Use budget-friendly bedding plants as fill-ins.

- Purchase plants locally to save on shipping, but shop mail-order catalogs for an extensive selection and specials. Choose reputable plant purveyors that offer a guarantee for replacement or money back.

plant shopping
above left: At the nursery or garden center, group plants as you might place them in your garden. Survey the collection with an eye for color and texture. Mix and match plants to please the eye and meet site requirements.

adding plants

plantscaping wisdom

Select plants to populate your garden rooms with color, fragrance, and a seasonally changing backdrop. Assess your planting space and surrounding living areas and decide if, for instance, you want plants for color, noise muffling, privacy, or shade. In cozy garden rooms, narrow planting beds often skirt the edges of the space, promising little room for roots. In this case, grow up. Use trellises, vines, wall planters, and hanging baskets to create a lush and beautiful view.

Containers eke out garden space in areas thick with hardscape. Choose pots with looks that rival the plants filling them, particularly if you have room for only a few containers. Use saucers to protect surfaces beneath pots. For accents, perch character-rich garden art sparingly among confined beds or a container garden. Do not plunge into purchasing plants until you have a plan in hand, especially when filling lilliputian-size gardens. Otherwise, you may overbuy.

tight fix
above right: **Combine colorful flowers, wall-hugging vines, and hanging baskets to groom a garden that's short on space but long on looks.**

perennial pleasures
right: **In this walled garden, perennial plantings come and go with the seasons, lending themselves to viewing up close to savor their beauty.**

potted gardens

left: Containers keep gardens going strong in rooms where cramped quarters prevent lavishly expansive planting beds. Arrange pots to add visual punch to a setting, clustering them in odd-numbered groups. Display showy ornamental containers by placing them at the center of attention: as sentries at the entrance of a room, flanking a seating area, or standing at the front edge of flower beds. Within the garden, elevate a large pot on a pedestal, on a tree stump, on a concrete block, or on an overturned pot.

decorating

focus on style

Art and color give an outdoor room its personality. Craft a memorable garden room by arranging it around a theme. A *sala* (Spanish for living room), captures the character and comfort of a Mexican courtyard. Each element of the *sala*, from the adobe brick to the mesquite woodwork to the authentic Mexican accents, helps make this an alfresco living space that suits its desert home.

Create your outdoor sanctuary with equally inspired details. Look beyond the architecture of your house and consider your family's hobbies, favorite vacation spots, or cultural heritage when choosing a style for your garden room. Choose artwork, fabrics, and plants to enrich the look. Research your topic thoroughly, engaging the entire family in the project. For access to more great information, visit the hub of our gardening resources at **www.bhg.com/bkgarden**

quick-and-easy decor

Display artful accents to enhance your garden room's style and make it more interesting.

- **maximize the mystery:** Tuck accents into nooks so that all of your artful focal points aren't visible with a quick glance.

- **make it match:** Choose garden art that fits your room's color scheme pleasingly. Cover eyesores. Use sculpture to conceal bare spots in the garden or unwanted views.

- **light it right:** Sunlight glistens on a fountain or a sculpture during the day. For nighttime glitter, add lights or candles for supplemental illumination.

desert refreshment

right: A garden *sala*, or living room, blends the best of indoors and outdoors in a Mexican-style courtyard. Plantings support the theme, featuring potted palms, desert plants, and bright and colorful tropical bloomers.

wall art
left: Choose style-wise accessories. A mural on the fireplace enhances the *sala* theme.

living history
below left: When selecting a design motif, research relevant architectural elements, such as a Mayan-inspired fountain.

materially yours
below: Terra-cotta and stone, common in Mexican decor, combine in this outdoor room.

the elements

define the design elements

Well-planned garden rooms provide places for you to live comfortably and to manage the necessary details of daily life. Rooms also separate outdoor living areas from functional but not-so-pretty spaces, such as a compost pile, the trash can nook, or a stack of firewood. How you segue from hardworking areas to garden hideaways depends on your personal tastes and your family's needs. **styled to suit** Use childhood remembrances of favorite family vacation spots, lazy summer afternoons, or gardening with grandparents to stir the pot of personal style, letting the past spice up the present with the flavor of familiar themes. Rely on cultural heritage, historical interests, or architectural styles to inspire other motif ideas for your outdoor sanctuary plans.

building blocks Weave a unified tapestry of delineated spaces into a cohesive landscape by choosing components (walls, floors, ceilings, windows, doors, and such) and threading them into the overall design with thoughtful planning. The key design elements shown on the following pages help define space and style. But it's not enough to know that you need a wall to form an enclosure, for example. You want to understand where to place that wall, as well as what building materials would best suit the space and its uses.

If walls won't work into your design scheme, contain your room with an overhead covering instead. A tree, a canopy, or a vine-draped pergola forms a ceiling that instantly defines a garden space. Add furnishings and you have a room.

Next thing you know, you'll be planning for views and access to your garden rooms. Determine how much privacy and weather resistance the rooms require. Connect areas using practical paths or pergola-covered walkways.

details add distinction Use structures and plantings to make transition zones that link outdoor rooms or form indoor-outdoor areas. A bench-bedecked arbor (*opposite*) forms a basic entryway and transforms the area into a welcoming, livable space.

Complete your garden rooms with decorative elements. Outdoor fabrics offer comfort and maximize any style statement (vintage, Old World, or tropical, for instance). Lighting enhances security, safety, and outdoor livability.

floors: brick

cost	make it	skill
$$	2 days	easy

you will need

- stakes and string
- pickax
- spade
- landscape fabric
- gravel
- builder's sand
- plastic edging
- 10–inch–long steel spikes (⅜–inch diameter)
- bricks or pavers
- rubber mallet
- two 2×4s
- one 1×12
- heavy scrap boards and nails
- broom
- garden hose

brick island

Incorporate a hard–surface floor into a garden area to make an instant room. Flooring gives furniture firm footing as well. With a seating ensemble in place, your garden begs to host starlit suppers, morning coffee, and kick–back weekend brunches.

Bricks or concrete pavers promise patterns aplenty. Customize your patio with a personalized design. For your first project, choose a pattern that highlights the angular nature of bricks, laying them in straight or gently curving patterns (cutting bricks with a diamond or wet saw takes practice).

For the best brick bargain, locate clean, salvaged bricks, or you'll invest energy in chipping away clinging mortar. New brick pavers rank as moderately expensive among flooring options, but their durability justifies the cost.

dining in the round

right: **A brick floor forms an ideal basis for a garden room.**

1 define the edges To construct a brick patio, begin by defining the patio shape with stakes and string. Use a pickax and spade to excavate enough soil to fit a 5-inch-deep base plus the thickness of a brick. Line the area with landscape fabric. Add and compact gravel to form a 4-inch base. Top gravel with 1 inch of builder's sand, leaving a slightly raised crown in the center of the area to allow for settling. Anchor plastic edging with steel spikes. Set border bricks into place.

2 lay the bricks Tamp sand with a handmade tamper fashioned by nailing heavy boards to the end of a 2×4. Begin to lay the bricks along an edge. Fit bricks together snugly; gently tamp them in place and level, using a rubber mallet. As you work, kneel on a 1×12 board laid on top of the bricks to avoid disturbing the level bricks and sand base. Level disturbed sand, if necessary, using the edge of a 2×4. Keep the site covered with a tarp if it rains during construction.

3 finish the job Toss handfuls of builder's sand over the finished brick floor. Working from one side to the other, use a stiff broom to sweep sand over the bricks until the cracks are filled. Water with a fine mist from a garden hose. Repeat the process a week after construction and whenever bricks wobble.

floors: stained concrete

cost	make it	skill
$-$$$	weekend	easy

you will need

- concrete stain
- concrete cleaner
- scrub brush
- rubber gloves
- knee pads
- manual pump sprayer
- tarps or old sheets
- paintbrush (optional)
- sealant (optional)

concrete cover-up

If your dreams of a garden room include a spacious floor, concrete combines affordability with long-lasting durability in any climate. Use stain to soften concrete's harshness and create a warm look.

Concrete coloring options abound. For a soon-to-be-poured concrete area, purchase a powdered dye to mix into wet concrete. With this approach, as the masonry wears, newly exposed surfaces show a consistent color. If your concrete came with your home, blend the nondescript gray into surrounding plantings using an easy staining technique, such as the one shown *opposite*. Some stains involve acid etching that initiates a chemical reaction between the staining solution and the concrete to fashion a colorfast surface. Other stains create a rich palette that mimics marble. Combining staining and etching techniques yields the look of cobblestone. Explore the options and browse color swatches at a local home improvement store or on the Internet before committing your concrete to one particular procedure.

color your world

right: Choose a concrete color that blends with surrounding plantings, structures, and furnishings. The concrete's terra-cotta tone complements the silver-blue of the table, chairs, and nearby foliage plants.

1 choose a color Concrete staining techniques work on individual pavers as well as on slabs. Stains may not hide concrete defects or discoloration, but cracks give the surface a weathered look. Remember that stains, like paint, appear darker when spread over a large area. Unify separate rooms by using hues in the same color family. Stain masonry surfaces (including upright ones) throughout your garden. Apply stain to existing surfaces or to new ones using the same techniques.

2 clean the concrete Tint existing masonry with a water-base stain that won't harm the environment. It will adhere only to clean, dry concrete. Use a concrete cleaner, following the manufacturer's directions. Typically, cleaning the concrete is the hardest part of this project, but it requires nothing more than a scrub brush and old-fashioned elbow grease. Wear rubber gloves and knee pads for protection. Allow cleaned surfaces to dry thoroughly before staining them.

3 begin to stain Before you start staining, dab a little on an inconspicuous spot to check the effect. Use a manual pump sprayer to apply stain. Protect surrounding surfaces, including plants, from donning a new hue by covering them with tarps or old sheets. Apply as many coats of stain as the manufacturer suggests. If you stain steps or vertical elements, such as concrete columns, trade the pump for a paintbrush for better results. Apply a sealant if you wish.

floors: recycled rubber

cost	make it	skill
$$$	afternoon	easy

you will need

- concrete cleaner and scrub brush
- recycled-rubber brick-look mats
- utility knife
- silicone-base weatherproof adhesive

recycled retreat

Camouflage an ordinary concrete slab with faux-brick mats. The magic of recycling transforms worn tires to produce the look of bricks with the resilience of rubber. The resulting floor casts a spell of luxurious ease. It doesn't retain heat like its true-to-life brick counterpart, and it cushions the blow when young ones take a tumble. Cool, cushioned, and comfortable on bare feet, recycled rubber mats offer a floor that's weather-worthy and geared for a growing family. The rubbery surface provides a nonfatiguing area for standing. It pays to look for new products and technology, especially if it results in money savings or the ideal finished look.

This floor treatment, instead of slippery tile, marries well with a spa or pool. Once you snug the mats into place, you're looking at a surface that lasts as long as concrete. Except for occasional sweeping and a rinse with the garden hose, the maintenance is nil.

Save money on this project by pouring the concrete slab base yourself. It's a big job. Research it first and line up help from a friend, preferably someone with concrete know-how.

brick look-alikes

right: Made from recycled rubber tires, 25×34-inch brick-look mats cover a concrete slab and give an alfresco family room a handsome, cushioned floor.

1 position the mats Using a concrete cleaner and a scrub brush, clean and dry the surface that the mats will cover; allow the surface to dry. Lay out the faux-brick mats, fitting them together snugly. Maintain the paver pattern as you lay the mats. When you have all the mats in position, check the pattern to make sure you positioned everything correctly. Have another person check the work at this point, too, especially if you will be gluing mats into place. Use a utlilty knife to trim edges where necessary.

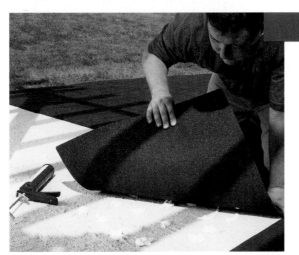

2 stick 'em down Gluing the recycled rubber mats is not necessary, although adhesive will hold the mats in place more securely. At the very least, plan to glue any small pieces to keep them in place. Ask the mat manufacturer or your local mat retailer to suggest an adhesive; otherwise, purchase a silicone-base weatherproof product. Test the glue on several small mat sections before using it on the entire patio.

3 complete the task If you are gluing all of the mats into place, apply adhesive to the largest pieces first; then tackle the smaller ones. It's easiest to lay straight-edge sections first. Work your way out toward rounded areas. Cut mats to fit snugly around any posts in your project area. Follow the adhesive manufacturer's recommendations for drying time before walking or setting furniture on the newly glued mat.

floors

mixed media

As you consider flooring options for your garden rooms, don't overlook the surest way to create a one-of-a-kind treatment: blending materials. Begin your quest for the ideal surface by taking an inventory of the materials that currently decorate your home's facade as well as any existing outdoor structures or surfaces that you plan to keep. Use this inventory to begin a list of potential hardscaping. Juxtapose possible combinations to create a plan for an outdoor floor that blends beautifully into your site.

If you prefer, choose flooring components that don't already appear on your property. Mix options according to your budget and the mood you want to create. Combine one surface with a less expensive one, such as stone with gravel or large concrete pavers with grass joints to create interesting effects and cut costs. Use small pavers to make small areas appear larger. With clever choices, you can make the floor the most attractive part of the space.

Trade living mortar for concrete when piecing together a stone-embroidered surface by using groundcovers to fill in cracks between stones. Ground-hugging beauties include Scotch moss, Irish moss, blue star creeper, and turf grasses, as well as creeping varieties of thyme, sedum, mint, and oregano. When planting greenery between stones, give it a good start. Water plants regularly and avoid stepping on them until root systems

dynamic duo
right: **Pair slate set in concrete with large, 4×4-foot exposed-aggregate pavers to craft an earthtone floor treatment that's attractive and enduring.**

take hold and plants begin to grow.

Whatever materials you choose to blend, start your floor by laying a solid foundation made to withstand your region's climate. The base for most flooring options is the same. Master the gravel-sand layering and compacting method (see page 37), and your options will be endless.

quilted terrace

above: A careful blending of Arizona flagstone, dark green Scotch moss, and light green Irish moss forms a pleasing patchwork patio.

diamonds are forever

left: Create a pebble and paver parquet for a playful but neat look. Keep the pea gravel (or mulch) in bounds with some kind of edging, such as the cedar strips here.

floors

paving primer

The right surface underfoot transforms an uninspiring corner of your yard into a destination. Choose a material that complements your house and the garden room. Keep durability at the top of your checklist as you shop for materials. Remember that long-lasting surfaces requiring little upkeep cost more at the outset but save money in the long run. Research installation techniques for materials that catch your eye. Figure out what will require professional help; include the logistics and cost of material delivery in that assessment. Factor these items into your project budget.

mix and match

right: Flagstone hobnobs easily with other materials and looks great. Whether you lay the floor or hire a pro to do it, splash color into the scene with china dish shards or handcrafted tiles.

brick & tile Cost-wise, new bricks add up, especially for a sizable area. Salvaged bricks typically command a lower price and come with a rich patina. Select bricks rated for your climate, installing them on a bed of compacted gravel topped with sand (see page 37). Don't mortar brick in northern regions; freeze-thaw cycles crack both surfaces. As a floor covering, tile's beauty is unrivaled. Use it cost effectively by tucking individual tiles as accents into other floor treatments. Select tile that's designed for outdoor use, steering clear of slick finishes. To decrease cold-weather-induced cracks, use unglazed quarry tile with a water absorption rate of less than 5 percent.

stone Materials classified as flagstone include limestone, slate, granite, marble, and sandstone. Visit a quarry and handpick your flagstone, paying by weight or by the piece. Irregular-shape stones are lower priced than custom-cut ones. Do not haul the flagstone from the quarry unless your vehicle is designed to carry heavy loads and you have the strength to unload it. Focus on native stone for your floor needs; stones harvested in far-flung locales earn their price in shipping fees. Flagstone lends an informal tone to any setting, especially when it's not fitted tightly together like a jigsaw puzzle. Fill cracks between stones with creeping plants, gravel, or mortar.

pavers The advantages of precast concrete pavers range from good looks and long-lasting wear to color selection and wide availability. Best of all, pavers withstand freeze-thaw cycles. Interlocking pavers won't dislodge individually, creating tripping hazards. Add pavers to your landscape using a dry-installation technique (much like the brick patio on page 37). Choose pavers with high strength ratings. Look for a lifetime guarantee; some manufacturers offer it. Avoid pavers containing iron aggregate, because they may rust over time. Visit a stone yard or home improvement store to peruse the paver shape selection available before drafting your floor pattern from a variety of design possibilities.

walls: bamboo trellis

cost	make it	skill
$	1 day per panel	easy

wall decor

Walls produce instant privacy, a basic tenet for creating a garden room. View a wall as a blank canvas begging for color and add that color courtesy of garden art, collectible displays, or skyward-scampering vines. Our easy-to-build bamboo panels weave a touch of Asia into any room and do double-duty as trellises.

Make quarter-rounds by cutting each bamboo pole in half lengthwise, then cutting each piece in half lengthwise again. Set aside four 8-foot-long bamboo quarters for frame rails. Cut two of the remaining bamboo quarters into 3-foot-long pieces for vertical frame rails and one 2-foot-long piece for a shorter strip.

Build each frame by arranging two 3-foot and two 8-foot bamboo quarters in a rectangle, with ends overlapping. Place the remaining 3-foot and 8-foot bamboo quarters on top of this frame to form the front of the structure. Drill a $\frac{1}{8}$-inch hole through the ends of each piece where they intersect at the corners. Wire the pieces together only at the four corners. Adjust the rectangle until it's straight.

fence finery

right: **Dress up a plain wooden fence with latticework panels. This project makes wall trellises from bamboo strips but could just as easily use prefabricated latticework for the construction.**

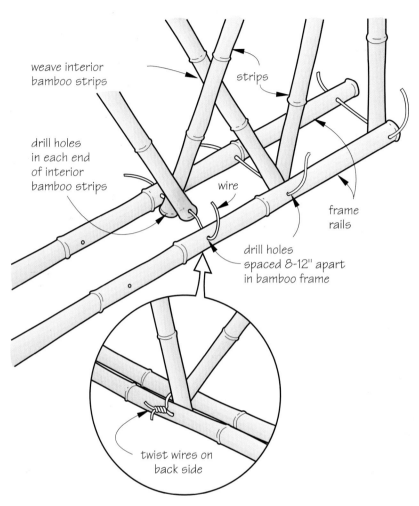

weave interior bamboo strips

strips

drill holes in each end of interior bamboo strips

wire

frame rails

drill holes spaced 8-12" apart in bamboo frame

twist wires on back side

Cut the remaining 8-foot bamboo quarters into 4-foot strips. Insert several diagonally and parallel to one another, about 6 inches apart, between the front and rear frames. Roughly size, cut, and add shorter diagonal strips near the frame corners to fill out the lattice design. Insert the remaining diagonal pieces in the opposite direction, using an over-under basket-weaving technique. The ends of opposing diagonals should intersect one another at the frames. Drill ⅛-inch holes at these intersecting points, and wire the layers of bamboo together. Use screws to mount your panel to a fence or wall.

walls

strong and silent

In the garden, walls create enclosure in one area and enhance a sense of openness in another. Place your walls strategically to shape a sanctuary.

Aim for privacy that's complete or partial, depending on your needs. For example, a spa or pool calls for a higher level of seclusion than a play area or a dining room.

Position walls to separate an area but allow accessibility. Before adding a wall, consider all views extending to and from the proposed enclosure; avoid blocking views.

Choose a good-neighbor wall design that looks acceptable from either side, although both sides need not appear the same. If the wall edges your property, confirm the property line and any easement restrictions before building. Determine building code and permit requirements that may affect the wall's height and construction method.

Avoid making a harsh, prisonlike wall by adding elements of interest to it. Decorate the flat surface of a wall using construction techniques, such as a stucco treatment, tile inserts, carved niches, or cutout windows. Incorporate a fountain, lighting, or hanging planters when building the wall, including the necessary hardware or electrical elements in its construction.

wall flowers at work

right: **When building a stacked-stone wall, tuck soil pockets between rocks for plants that will thrive there, including alpine varieties of dianthus, armeria, draba, and sedum.**

sculptural detail
above: Embellish a stucco or adobe privacy wall with raised details. The chevron design, made by setting molds into the wall and covering them with stucco, is echoed in the wooden gate's construction.

flowery finesse
left: Garden walls offer great decorative potential. Fit your walls with a fountain, a birdbath, planters, or artful plaques.

walls: wood & copper fence

creative corral

A fence defines garden room boundaries in a decorative way that's typically more open to air flow and less expensive than a wall. The height of the fence depends on your goal. Privacy dictates fences be at least head high, but traffic flow on adjacent sidewalks and intersections calls for structures between knee and waist high.

Combine design, construction materials, and paint or stain color to build a not-too-confining barrier that's a handsome landscape backdrop. A mixture of solid board panels, lattice, copper pipes, and window planting shelves give this fence (*right*) a distinctive style that lets light and air flow through while partially obstructing views of passersby.

The effectiveness of a fence depends on its positioning too. This one wraps around part of a front yard, screening the driveway and sidewalk. As climbing roses mature and drape the fence, it appears more and more to have sprouted in place.

Before you build, consider using fence-post anchors that enable you to install fence posts temporarily or permanently without digging holes or pouring concrete. Instead, you drive a hollow spike into the ground and stand a post in it.

blended fence

right and *below:* The cedar fence suits the brick cottage and perennial gardens that it shields. Narrowly spaced copper pipes produce the look of shutters. Sheets of copper cover plant ledges that offer a window to the world.

setting a fence post

1 dig Lay out the site using stakes and strings; mark post placement with stakes. Use cedar or pressure-treated wood for bottom rails (2×4s) and posts (4×4s or 6×6s). Set posts 6 to 8 feet apart, depending on the size of the fence sections that you build or buy. Use a (rented) posthole digger or an auger to make the holes 2 feet deep. Cover the bottom of the holes with 6 inches of gravel and insert the posts. Check each post for plumb, using a level. Nail temporary braces to hold the posts in place.

2 fill Mix quick-set concrete according to the manufacturer's instructions. Shovel concrete into the hole around the post, taking care not to bump the post. Have a helper tamp the concrete, using a broom handle or wood scrap to remove air bubbles. Round off the top of the concrete above the soil line; mounding the concrete allows water to drain away from the post. Let the concrete set at least 24 hours before hanging the lower fence rails, otherwise you might force the posts out of alignment.

3 hang Attach the bottom fence rails to the posts. Choose a less expensive grade of rot-resistant lumber for the upper rails and fencing. Join rails to posts using galvanized rail clips. Purchase hot-dip galvanized hardware to reduce rust. Use a string and line level and a combination square to ensure that each rail is level and square with the posts. Paint or stain posts, rails, and fencing before nailing or screwing fencing in place.

walls

fence finery

Choose a fence style that suits both your home and garden, blending the two in an architecturally cohesive way. The style of fencing you choose depends largely on the purpose of the barrier. For instance, a solid fence promises long-lasting privacy, while a row of vinyl pickets offers an opportunity to build an easy-care, decorative barrier. Craft pickets from fruit tree prunings or another material that's handy and relevant to your garden room's style. Posts and rails alone make a simple, rustic divider.

Change the look of traditional fencing by using bold-hue paint or stain. Use the same method to turn a usually formal wrought-iron fence into an electric-blue (or -red or -yellow) wonder.

Push the limits of boundary building by combining wooden fences and masonry walls to create hardworking structural elements in the landscape. Concrete or stone constructions allow you to include a pizza oven, grill, fireplace, or fountain. Or intermingle architectural structures with sections of living fence.

Top your fence with lattice strips to heighten the level of privacy and style (*right*). Add finishing touches to posts. Top them with finials, from concrete acorns or copper caps to wooden pyramids or spheres.

aspire higher

right: **Disguised as a raised planter, a retaining wall reaches new heights when its design includes a fireplace, flue, and fencing. The stucco fireplace makes the patio a favored place. Latticework atop the fence adds visual interest and reduces a stockade effect.**

fence bends

left: Curved-rail fencing cuts an artful swath around established trees and flower beds. Use vinyl or recycled lumber to eliminate painting.

salvage style

below left: Reusing parts from two old fences and interspersing the two styles of pickets yields a fresh look. The stone-topped posts add personality.

wood wellness

You have options for finishing wooden garden structures to seal and protect them from weather. Finishes affect the look of the wood and its maintenance.

- **water repellant:** Including fungicide; protects structures from weather as wood turns gray over time; lasts up to 2 years.

- **paint:** Exterior grade in vast color choices; requires priming and reapplication every 3 to 5 years.

- **penetrating stain:** Mildew-resistant; includes color and lasts up to 10 years between applications without priming.

- **transparent stain:** With ultraviolet inhibitor; enhances the wood's natural color up to 2 years.

walls: living fence

cost	make it	skill
$$	3 growing seasons	easy

you will need

- three or more dwarf fruit trees
- posthole digger (optional)
- 4×4 posts
- 2×4 top rail (8 feet long)
- 14-gauge wire
- hand pruners
- cloth-covered wire plant ties

especially espalier

Train dwarf fruit trees using standard pruning techniques to form a living wall and enjoy the privacy and fresh produce it yields. In an espalier (pronounced es-PAL-yay), plants grow along a usually flat, symmetrical framework against a wall, trellis, or freestanding form. Frequent pruning and tying of new growth directs plants into a rigid pattern, such as intersecting diamonds (*right*) or horizontal arms or elbows.

Research patterns and plan your espalier to fit your needs. The traditional Belgian fence (shown *right*) forms an airy, artistic barrier. Use espalier to convert narrow planting beds along driveways or walls into productive gardens. For espalier fruit fences, choose dwarf varieties of apples, peaches, or pears. Train a purely ornamental fence by choosing a blooming tree or shrub, such as flowering crabapple, magnolia, or double-file viburnum.

edible walls

right and *far right:* Select fruit tree varieties that boast disease resistance, such as 'Jonafree' apples, to create a more carefree fence. Other great apple choices include 'MacFree' and 'Freedom'.

1 support Select an overall pattern for your espalier. Build an appropriate framework of stout posts (8 feet apart), a top rail, and heavy-gauge wire horizontal supports. Stretch wire tautly from post to post, spaced vertically at 1-foot intervals, to create a framework. If you train trees against a wall, leave 12 inches between the structure and the support system to allow for maintenance and air circulation. Plant 2- or 3-year-old dwarf trees at least an arm's length apart.

2 anchor Make planting holes at least twice the diameter of the plant's root ball. Plant trees slightly in front of the wire supports. Refill the planting holes and water thoroughly. Water young trees weekly during their first summer and fall if rain is lacking. Cut off branches extending to the back or front; leave branches reaching to the sides. If you train trees along a wall, position a nail or an eye hook in the wall near intersecting branches. Loosely twist a plant tie around the branches and the hook.

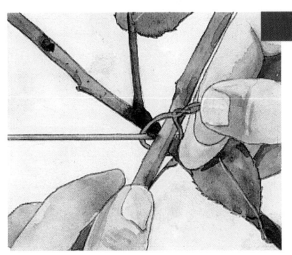

3 train Crisscross branches from neighboring trees to train them into the desired pattern. Twist a plant tie around the branches and the wire to secure them, leaving room for branch growth. Over the next three or so years, prune and train trees in late winter. As the trees grow, continue to cross and tie the branches to the framework, snipping unwanted growth to maintain the pattern. Remove fruit buds the first two years to concentrate the tree's energy in growing branches. Look for fruit in the third year.

lattice

classic camouflage

When it comes to garden cover-ups, lattice reigns as a popular and classic choice. Standing solo or swathed in vines, a section of latticework effectively hides, surrounds, or otherwise encloses elements in the garden. Whether concealing air-conditioning units or trash cans, lattice lavishes stylistic charm over the unsightly necessities of life. Tacked onto the sides of a prefabricated garden shed, latticework dresses up dullness while providing the perfect place to hang tools.

Whatever your garden's style, lattice blends form and function. Choose from prefabricated, 4×8-foot panels available in a variety of patterns at lumberyards or home centers. Or turn your creativity loose to construct homemade panels of lath or bamboo. Either way, use the lacy network of woven strips to make decorative screens that limit the view without blocking it.

When shaping garden rooms, use lattice to form boundaries that let in breezes and sunshine. This may be a big plus in a small area with limited exposure. Use latticework screens to surround a dining nook or encircle a spa. Hide utility meters behind an appropriate-size framed panel.

The peekaboo structure of lattice enhances mystery in the garden, especially when draped in vines. Smother a lattice panel with annual flowering vines or establish perennial climbers, such as hops, clematis, trumpet vine, or climbing hydrangea, to soften the sections with concealing foliage.

screened scene

right: **Vinyl lattice panels, topped with a curved rail and detailed pergola, conceal a family's backyard living room. A tangle of morning glory vines flourishes on the structure.**

1 garden weave

Garden-style lattice features 3-inch openings. This pattern provides more privacy when vines scramble up and over the panels. Use this lattice as a support or windbreak for plants or for added privacy.

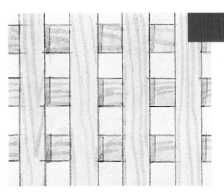

2 vertical and horizontal

Choose a lattice pattern and size based on your intended use. For a carport, 6-inch-wide openings let plenty of light and air through. Conceal garbage cans or a compost pile using lattice with a smaller opening size, such as 1½ inches.

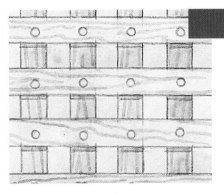

3 circles and squares

Latticework styles and their decorative effects vary. Customize a standard grid by drilling holes at the points where strips intersect. Use this lattice in areas that require airflow, such as in narrow passageways or damp courtyards.

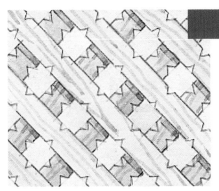

4 notched

A star-shape illusion results when notched lattice strips come together to create a panel with a designer touch. Purchase prefabricated panels crafted with notched strips, or customize them by shaping strips and cobbling your own stylized motif.

lattice

woven wonders

Enhance the purpose of your garden room and the pleasures you find in it with carefully placed panels of wood or vinyl lattice. Use them as freestanding screens to divide space. Lattice added to structures helps form private retreats with an architectural sense of enclosure. Use lattice to enclose the sides of an entry arch or arbor and include a bench in the scheme. Attach woven panels to a potting bench frame to make it do double duty as a buffet.

Vinyl lattice offers flexibility, making it possible to shape a structure with a gracefully arched roof or a curved wall.

open-air room

right: Backed with a lattice wall, a pergola offers a shady and inviting retreat. The cut-out window adds a significant architectural detail.

airy alcove

above: Build a shady but airy retreat by cutting lattice panels to enclose a garden arbor. Leave the arch bare or train vines to twine over it.

wood or vinyl?

Wood is no longer the only lattice option. Consider vinyl products for durability with no maintenance. Traditional wood weathers to a silvery gray or perhaps dons an appealingly flaking coat of paint. Vinyl comes in several colors. It expands and contracts with temperature changes. Research vinyl products through local distributors. Work with vinyl as you would with wood, using a scroll saw and drill to cut and fit pieces together.

lattice: building a latticework screen

1   build the frame A lattice screen works hard in the garden. Use it as a privacy panel, a fence section, or the wall of an outdoor structure. Set the posts in place for your screen (see page 51), with spacing determined by the planned panel size. Build a frame of 2×4s, using weather-resistant cedar or pressure-treated lumber. Lay the frame on a flat surface, such as a driveway. Square each corner using a framing square, and insert temporary wooden braces to keep everything in place. Use galvanized nails to fasten the frame together at each corner.

2   reinforce the corners Remove each of the corner braces one at a time, checking each corner again with the framing square before securing the joint. Choose either a metal strap or angle to anchor the corners. Use only galvanized screws and hardware to minimize rusting as the frame weathers.

3   set the stops Place the frame on a sturdy raised surface, such as a pair of sawhorses. Cut pieces of 1×1-inch lumber to fit inside the frame and create stops for the lattice to rest on. Align the stop with one edge of the frame, and predrill holes at 1-foot intervals. Attach the stop to the inner side of the frame by driving screws through the 1×1 into the frame. Attach all four stops.

make good choices Buy **4** prefabricated lattice panels or build them with lath strips. First, compare prices between prefabricated sections and the materials necessary to construct the same-size sections. Ready-made 4×8-foot panels typically cost less. Inspect latticework carefully before purchasing it. Choose thicker cedar or pressure-treated latticework for its durability; thinner, less expensive panels are made with flimsy staples. With a brush or sprayer apply a wood-preserving finish to the latticework. Seal panel ends too. If you plan to apply a finish to the frame and stops, do so now.

attach the lattice After the finish **5** dries, lay the latticework on top of the frame's stops. Attach the lattice to the stops using a staple gun. Place a second set of stops on top of the latticework. Install the stops, following the same procedure as in step 3 (*opposite*).

attach the frame Fasten the frame **6** to the posts using galvanized lag screws spaced about 1 foot apart. Predrill holes and, for a neater appearance, countersink them. Fit each lag screw with a washer before driving it. If you painted or stained the frames, touch up around the screws after attaching them.

ceilings

over the top

What's the surest way to transform an area of the garden into a room? Cap it with a ceiling. Coverings for garden retreats range from the strictly architectural to a soft canopy of fabric or foliage.

Think about how you intend to use the room before determining the ceiling's style, allowing for sunbeams and starlight or for keeping out the weather. If you plan to fill the room with cozy-cushioned furniture, you'll want more substantial coverage than if you outfit the space with a weather-worthy teak or shorea furniture ensemble. A simple pergola provides an easy-to-build covering for a room. Plant vines at the base of the posts to form a living ceiling.

garden getaway

above: Gently arched beams and 2×2s form
a slatted roof that tempers the midday sun and
allows glimpses of sky and trees. Posts and
railings edge an 8-foot-square wooden deck.
Architectural details, such as the capitals and
keystone, echo trim on the house.

blooming abandon

left: A simple pergola, crowned with a tangle
of soft pink bougainvillea, encloses a garden
room that's rich with personality. Teak benches
invite lingering, and a flagstone floor keeps
feet dry on dewy mornings. Roses fill the room
with scent.

ceilings: awning

colorful canopy

Now you see it; now you don't. That's the story of a retractable awning. Fully extended, it casts cooling shade; rolled up, it permits sunshine to splash freely onto the patio and into interior rooms.

A retractable awning helps control light levels on a sun-exposed side of a house and saves energy costs. It also protects interior furnishings from sun-induced fading. Equipped with a motorized, tubular frame and internal wiring that runs into the house, the awning moves at the touch of a switch, extending to its full or partial potential.

Select awning fabrics that complement your home's architectural style and facade. If you want the awning to serve as a flashy focal point, lean toward bright tones. For a canopy that blends beautifully into the surroundings, choose hues that echo exterior shades found in the house color, trim, or shingles. Select fabric patterns proportionate to the size of your house and the awning. Small stripes look busy on a large expanse of fabric, while wide-stripe patterns overwhelm small homes. Stylish touches, such as contrasting trim, scalloped or keyhole valances, or tassels, perk up a solid-tone awning. Peruse your awning contractor's portfolio to view style and fabric options that look good on homes similar to yours.

roof on the move

above right: **Retract a motorized awning when you want to increase the light indoors or during high winds. This retracted awning fits snugly against the house.**

made in the shade

right: **Measuring 10×25 feet, this awning fits neatly over the recessed front entryway and creates a welcoming, shaded room.**

courtyard style

left: The heavy-duty fabric awning extends over a cozy seating area. When the retractable canopy was installed, a flagstone and gravel floor was added along with a table, chairs, and fragrant perennials to create an outdoor living room. The striped awning coordinates with the trim color of the house. As with most custom-made awnings, the tubular steel framework, weatherproof fabric, and operating mechanism were installed by the manufacturer.

garden rooms | **65**

ceilings: vine canopy

sheltering leaves

Train vines to weave a living ceiling anywhere in your garden that you desire shelter: between the house and the garage, over a patio or a deck, or in any area that could benefit from added shade. To begin, build a framework for the vines to climb and cover. Set posts (or brackets) into place for uprights; connect them with side rails. Run multistrand steel wires between the rails, forming a scaffold. Determine a pattern for the canopy based on the degree of coverage you want. For a long-lived ceiling, use perennial vines: climbing hydrangea, trumpet vine, ivy, wisteria, or clematis. In warmer climes, plant bougainvillea, jasmine, sky vine, or cat-claw creeper. Choose vines appropriate to your region's climate and the site's sun exposure.

leafy ceiling

left: A driveway between two historic Boston buildings needed shade. The owner wanted to spruce up the overhead space between the apartment buildings while preserving their architecture. To create a living roof, she planted three wisteria vines. The vines scrambled up to iron brackets along the sunny side of one of the buildings and twined their way across multistrand steel wires. It took four years for wisteria growth to cover the grid. Annual trimming requires a stepladder, a sharp pair of hand pruners, and a good sense of balance.

romance in bloom

left: The delightfully fragrant and colorful blooms of wisteria dangle from vines like clusters of grapes. The secret to a rich crop of flowers is properly timed pruning. Late-summer or early-fall pruning in cold climates gives vines ample time to set flower buds for the following spring. Prune during winter in warm climates.

entries: arbor

cost	make it	skill
$$	2 days	moderate

you will need

- shovel
- two 4×4 posts (11 feet long)
- gravel
- concrete
- two 2×6 crossbeams (6 feet long)
- stepladder
- framing square
- eight galvanized lag screws
- ratchet
- jigsaw
- two 2×6s (7 feet long)
- hammer
- galvanized nails
- twenty-six 2×2 rails (45 inches long)
- exterior-grade stain or paint

artful entry

Of all the useful garden structures, arbors offer modest scale and endless style variations. They fulfill many functions in the garden, beautifully framing a view, creating a private hideaway, or defining a path. Joined with fencing, an arbor shapes a classic garden entry. When coupled with a swing or bench, an arbor beckons for solitary reflection or intimate moments.

Consider views through the arbor in both directions when choosing its location. In a large garden, install an arbor partway down a path to invite visitors to explore what lies beyond. In a small garden, use an arbor to create an impression that the garden extends beyond it.

Choose a style that blends into the surrounding plantings and rooms. For durability, select an arbor crafted from pressure-treated wood, metal, or plastic. Use the materials list and instructions to make an arbor similar to the one pictured.

grand entrance

right: **If the arbor is near your house, select a construction material and design that complement your home's architecture.**

1 posts Dig holes for posts. Space the posts no more than 6 feet apart. (If you want to extend the distance, increase the beam size to 2×8.) Pour 6 inches of gravel in the holes, insert posts, and fill with concrete (see page 51). Cut two 6-foot-long 2×6s into four 3-foot-long crossbeams. They will define the depth of the arbor. Standing on a stepladder, use lag screws to secure the 2×6s to both sides of each post. Use a framing square to align the crossbeams with the posts before tightening the screws.

2 beams Shape the decorative detail at the ends of the 7-foot-long 2×6 beams using a jigsaw. Design an end treatment to match your home's architecture or other structures in the garden. Attach the beams to the crossbeams by driving at least two galvanized nails through the 2×6s into the ends of the crossbeams. You'll need help with this step. Have your partner hold the loose end of each 2×6 until you nail it into position. Cut and install optional arching crosspieces.

3 rails Cut 2×2 rails to length. Position the first one carefully, then drive one nail through each end of the rail into the 2×6 beams beneath. Lay an extra piece of 2×2 against the first rail to determine spacing for the next and subsequent rails; ensure that each rail extends equally over the beams before nailing. Stain or paint the arbor either before or after constructing it. Plant vines, such as climbing roses, honeysuckle, or jasmine, to cloak the arbor with fragrance.

entries: doors

open sesame!

In a house, a door stands as a sentry of sorts, providing security. In the garden, however, it serves mostly to welcome, suggesting greater discoveries lie beyond its threshold. Decide if your garden room merits a door by asking yourself several questions: Do you desire a room that's enriched with seclusion? Do you wish to exclude a view altogether? Do you need to secure an area?

A door beckons when it's open, but when closed, it's a firm warning to peering eyes and wandering feet: Keep out unless invited in. If you don't wish to block a view altogether, site a door to diminish a view. In this way, a door enhances a room's sense of mystery, revealing only a hint of what lies beyond while withholding a portion for visitors. For certain outdoor amenities, such as a pool, pond, or spa, municipal codes may require a secure enclosure. In that case, a door provides necessary access to your outdoor room while conforming to codes.

When selecting a door, choose construction and materials that complement the style of your garden room and that blend with nearby structures. Consider future maintenance needs, such as painting, staining, or replacing parts. Hang a door with weather-worthy hardware, and keep hinges and latches oiled for easy opening.

secret garden

right: A pair of painted doors set into a wall help transform a courtyard garden into a colorful hideaway. Scout doors at salvage stores, flea markets, auctions, or estate sales. For a formal garden, choose ornate metalwork or dark-stained wooden doors. Distressed wood suits a cottage garden such as this one.

room divider

left: Situate a door to delineate adjoining garden rooms and to frame a picturesque view from either side. To use this kind of entry most effectively, reinforce it on either side with a border of some sort, such as a fence, a wall, or a hedge. The path continues the beguiling nature of this transition by leading through the entry and bending out of sight in the distance. Keeping the underfoot surface the same threads the two rooms together with a sense of continuity. The potted plants accentuate and soften the doorway, making it more welcoming.

peekaboo door

left: A latticework door and panel link a security fence to the deck at the back of this house, framing the entry to the outdoor room while limiting access to it. The lattice also allows see-through views.

entries: gates

through the garden gate

An effective garden gate demands forethought. The right blend of materials and design welcomes guests without surrendering your sense of security. Aim to blend or contrast the gate with the site. For high-traffic, main-entrance gates, consider durability as well as decorative details. Wrought iron promises low maintenance and long wear, while wooden entries require restaining or repainting over time. For a natural look, bamboo boasts remarkable wear without upkeep; a rustic branch-and-twig structure offers charm at little cost but won't last a lifetime.

Top a gate with an arch to create a grand entrance. Install a self-locking latch and make a handy exit for the kids. Hang gates with weatherproof hardware and anchor them to sturdy posts for strength and endurance.

ornate gate

above right: An 8-foot-tall wrought-iron gate teams with an accompanying fence to present sophisticated security. Greenery blends the structures with the site and enhances privacy.

home sweet home

right: A waist-level gate in a picket fence suits a cottage-style house and garden and announces the point of entry. Paired with a clematis-covered arch, it's perfectly inviting.

stylish entrée

left: **Embellish the entry to your home and garden with a gable-top cedar gate. The double swinging doors allow a generous, 6-foot-wide entry—ample room to fit a couple of people or a garden cart through it. The gate design complements the fence motif. The roof affords shelter on inclement days and is an easy-to-add element for an existing gate. Install lighting near your gate and include climbing plants to complete the scene.**

entries

first impressions

An arbor, pond, and plentiful plantings turn every trip out the front door into a relaxing walk through a private garden. The structure frames the space, making an entry room and giving the house a more welcoming face.

Position the garden where it faces or flanks the front door. Plants emphasize and shelter the entry. If space permits, add seating and large potted plantings as finishing touches. Where the overall space is small, opt for open-air walls, such as latticework, which define the room without confining it.

design delight

right: **Substantial columns help match the front entry garden's architecture (in both style and size) with that of the house. The structure's airy walls of lattice bolster privacy and reflect the window patterns.**

courtyard charm

above: Each element of this entry garden blends with the theme of modern formality, from the marble-edge raised concrete pond to the decorative ornate planters filled with tree roses. The broad concrete path unfurls like an area rug with its scored and stained design.

wet escape

left: The sound of running water sets a relaxing mood in any garden, but its effect intensifies in a small space. Placing a water feature in a front door courtyard muffles nearby street noise. Fish splash in the pond, adding colorful movement to the scene.

entries

dooryard garden

Design an inviting entry room by changing the approach to your home from purely utilitarian to fancifully functional. Include a structure that anchors and defines the space, such as a pergola, an arbor, or a trellis. In the front door garden (at *right* and *opposite*), a pergola reduces the scale of the house, making the entryway a substantial garden room.

Mimic the architectural details, colors, and motifs of your home in any structure you add to your outdoor foyer. Let paths establish the access to your house,

welcome friends

right: **A profusion of plants transforms a dooryard's sterile concrete approach with layers of softening color and texture. The pergola relates the house to the garden, while adding a bit of shade and privacy.**

leading both feet and eyes. Select a surface that provides firm footing in all seasons. Help a standard 4-foot-wide path enhance a small house by flanking it with layered plantings. Place ground-hugging specimens near path edges; then stairstep plants behind them. If an entry path links to an adjoining space, such as a side yard or a walled garden, distinguish the public and private areas with a gate, an arch, or a door.

Focus on safety in your entrance design. Avoid obstructing walkways with pots, garden art, or overgrown plants. When siting trees, imagine them as mature specimens and give them plenty of growing room so they won't block the entry. Include night lighting that's appealing and unobtrusive. Lights outfitted with daylight sensors and motion detectors ensure safe access after dark.

walk this way
above left: Potted plants dress up the 3×5-foot concrete slabs and soften the entryway's overall look. Clusters of flowering plants add color. They can be switched easily as the seasons change and plants finish blooming.

unifying themes
left: A repeating pattern of concrete slabs ties together the driveway and garden entryway. The sturdy turfgrass between the slabs needs only occasional mowing. The huge driveway slabs sit on steel reinforcers with irrigation lines hidden under the turf.

windows

rooms with views

The elements of a garden room shape its personality. Whether a room's character is playful or precise, the addition of a window completes the style with sophistication. Windows work hard in the garden, interrupting the wall of a room and framing a view.

Take either a literal or figurative approach to the world of sashes and panes. Using literal windows in the garden means hanging sashes, complete with glass, in your outdoor oasis. Secure these homey accoutrements from sturdy supports by twisting eye bolts into the tops of the window frames to limit movement in gusty winds.

window to the wild

above: **Nothing captures attention outdoors like a window sash hanging free from a support. Place your see-through divider where it frames a view you want to see again and again.**

circular viewpoint

right: **Interrupt the monotony of an existing wooden fence with a spherical portal to a backyard paradise. This moon gate could be made of stone or brick and its opening might include shutters or a metal grille for privacy.**

In the figurative sense, windows function as portals to your garden, celebrating your garden's good looks by outlining favored vistas. Conceptual windows take many forms. The opening may occur as a simple break in a hedge or as an intricately defined shape in an existing wall or a latticework panel. Position the window to grant visual access to a section of the garden that's not part of your immediate room's surroundings. That visual slice of the garden becomes a work of living art, viewed through the frame of the window.

bordered beauty
above left: Create the suggestion of a window in an existing arbor, pavilion, or deck. Position it to capture a scene, such as a winding path, a water feature, or a sculptural focal point, that beckons guests into the garden.

glazed look
left: Salvage windows add personality to a garden room. Topped with a valance, the freshly painted sashes bring the cozy comfort of home to a deck or porch.

transitions

rites of passage

As you develop rooms in your garden, thoughtfully plan the transition areas between them. Paths offer the natural choice for joining separate rooms. Increase their effectiveness with decorative touches. Adopt a minimalist style for transitional decor, focusing on a few key elements, such as columns, arbors, or pots of flowers. If the dimensions permit, incorporate a bench into the transition area to establish it as a room in its own right.

If a passage runs 15 feet or longer, repeat architectural details over the course of the walk. A colonnaded walkway, a series of arbors, or a soldierly row of freestanding columns draw eyes and feet along a path that links neighboring rooms. Position a focal point at the end of a passage to lure guests to amble the entire length and reach the next room.

covered walkway

above right: A long, narrow passage becomes a stately walkway with the addition of a pergola. Colorful ground-level pots of flowers counterbalance the structures.

alluring passage

right: A series of arbors link adjoining garden rooms. Combined with a large-scale avenue, the structures create a dramatic vista.

serene scene

left: A courtyard, arranged at the bottom of a steep staircase, holds its own as a destination in addition to providing a transition between house and garden. A stone birdbath that is also a recirculating fountain provides a strong focal point.

fresh-air fantasy

Modern outdoor fabrics withstand high humidity, drenching downpours, and glaring sun without fading or disintegrating. Swaths of fabric soften structures while adding a graceful curve, an alluring fold, or a cascade of touchable beauty.

Work textiles into your outdoor-room plans and reap the rewards of comfort and style. Fabric panels dangling like banners form billowing walls. Suspended in gravity-defying trapeze-artistry fashion, a fabric ceiling provides a canopy perfect for shielding guests from bright sun or light rain. In a romantic hideaway (*right*), an easy-to-stitch hanging canopy provides privacy and shelter under branches and leaves. Opulent prints dress up a mundane outdoor table and cover cushions with verve. Slipcovers give everyday chairs an exotic look.

Find awning materials at fabric shops and outdoor furniture stores. Look for polyester, acrylic, or nylon fabrics that promise protection against ultraviolet light. Stitch your creations together with polyester or nylon thread, which is designed to withstand the elements.

table for two

right: Coordinated fabrics set the tone for a cozy getaway area. A wrought-iron candle chandelier and matching candlestands heighten the romantic mood. Open-air walls let the serenades of birds, bugs, and breezes flow through.

overhead hangups

Casting shade or catching raindrops, the fabric ceiling unfurls among the trees. Determine your canopy dimensions based on the size of your seating ensemble. Use a contrasting, heavy-duty fabric and sew a decorative edge that will help the canopy weather wind. Place nickel-plated grommets into each corner and hang the fabric from nylon rope attached to trees or tent stakes. Remove any leaf litter or twigs that fall onto the fabric from trees overhead.

sheer slipcover

Sheer netting slipcovers drape ordinary metal-frame garden chairs with formal fancy. Find mosquito netting (made for outdoor use) at fabric and bedding stores. Place 2 to 3 yards of fabric over each chair. Cut tiny slits in the netting and thread the seat cushion ties through the cuts; tie cushions to chair frames with snug bows.

a fetching sketch

Plan your outdoor retreat with a site in mind. Inventory the location, taking note of branches that might serve as supports for the canopy and overhead lighting. Employ tent poles or sturdy stakes to uphold ends of the canopy that lack limb braces. Change the atmosphere altogether by switching fabrics. Trade the tailored look for bold tropical prints or bright, angular south-of-the-border designs.

finishing touches: outdoor fabrics

1 **a stitch in time** Pamper yourself with creature comforts crafted from weather-worthy textiles. Choose fabrics according to projects, favoring blends made for outdoor use. For grill covers and table linens, choose soil- and stain-resistant materials for easy cleanup. Select lightweight fabrics for billowy curtains or graceful slipcovers. When edging curtains, skirting a workbench, or covering furniture, choose heavier textiles that hang straight and tend not to blow. Dark-color and patterned fabrics disguise dirt and stains easily. If you prefer solids, choose textured fabrics for pleasing results.

2 **pillow talk** Cover outdoor cushions in lively hued fabric that's made to resist moisture, stains, and mildew. Sew welt cord into the seams of pillows and cushions to improve their durability and give them a tailored look. Making cushion covers with zippers allows easy removal for washing. Select a nylon zipper over a metal one, which can corrode and stick. Or, for a nifty closure, install nickel-plated snaps. Stuff pillows with polyester fiberfill, which absorbs little moisture. Most cushions and pillows crafted with outdoor fabrics last for years. Extend that longevity by storing them under cover when not in use. If you want cushion ties to help keep them in place, sew two ties into the back corner seams of the cushion covers. Use either narrow strips of matching fabric or heavy ribbon to make the ties.

anchors away Invent your own easy-to-install pulley system to hang cloth draperies or screen and fabric panels (*left*) on a porch, deck, or other outdoor structure. First, make the panels by sewing a 4-inch-wide fabric edging onto 60-inch-wide fiberglass window screening (from a hardware store or home center). Screw hooks into a porch ceiling or overhead beams to suspend individual panels. Slip hooks through grommet holes you have punched into the panel or curtain corners with a grommet-making tool. Use nylon laundry line and sailboat pulleys to raise, lower, or draw back the drapes. To keep a panel or drape raised or gathered to one side, wrap the line around a cleat attached to a railing or the floor. Peruse a marine supply store for heavy-duty hardware such as pulleys and cleats, which are made to withstand the elements. Tuck weights into the bottom edging or hem of drapes to minimize their billowing when the wind blows.

on edge Experiment with different edging treatments as you plan your fabric accessories. A mitered corner, neatly sewn in a contrasting fabric, adds a formal touch to a tablecloth or floorcloth. Select oilcloth for table toppers or floor coverings, and you won't need to hem edges. Instead use pinking shears to cut geometric edges, such as zigzags or scallops. Stitch decorative trims to pillows that suit your room's style: Use nylon fringe, topstitching, rickrack, or leather seam binding. Hire a professional to make your outdoor fabric accessories if sewing isn't your forte.

finishing touches: lighting

lighten up

Set your garden room aglow with innovative, inexpensive lighting. Candles, strings of lights, and lanterns add as much appeal as a skyful of twinkling stars. The soft illumination casts a hypnotic spell that's conducive to evening entertaining and late-night conversations.

If your night-lighting choices include candles, explore display options and use materials that you have on hand. Line the center of a table with glass-footed compotes or sherbet dishes filled with votives. Give new life to canning jars by covering their bottoms with an inch or two of sand, small river rock, marbles, sea glass, or recycled glass; stand a small candle inside. Transform the jars into hanging lanterns by tightly wrapping wire around jar necks and twisting it to form a loop above the mouth of each jar. Burn citronella-scented candles for their reputed bug-repelling effects.

Shelter flames from wind by snuggling candles into deep containers or by slipping glass chimneys or patterned graters or colanders over lit candles.

Use oil lamps or lanterns whenever an evening calls for sustained lighting. Or rely on electric lights for hours-on-end illumination. String Chinese-style lanterns from gutters to light a walkway, taking care to purchase the right-size bulbs to fit inside the paper globes. Weave strings of twinkle lights around tree branches to add sparkle to the evening breeze. Outline a garden trellis, market umbrella, or fence with strings of lights to create a glimmering focal point. Nestle lights among garden flowers and foliage for a magical glow.

fiery flowers

right: Fashion a tabletop water garden that glows after dark. Float water lettuce plants in a large enamel pan. Tuck 2-inch-round candles or tea lights into the center of each plant. Other potential candleholders include tulips, roses, or other large floatable blooms. Snip off the stem and nestle a tealight within the flower petals.

Position lights where you want to illuminate potentially treacherous footing, such as around a deck, along a path, or beside stairs. Place lights near seating and dining areas, either above head or below eye level to avoid bumps and glare. Keep safety in mind when using candles; place them away from combustible items and beyond the reach of children and pets.

thrift store glow

left: **Secondhand fixtures include tapers standing in a sand-filled watering can, bud-vase-shaded string lights, and wineglasses topped with shades from old gas lamps.**

twinkle lights

Low-cost strings of lights become rich with character when you dress bulbs in homemade lampshades. Slightly enlarge the drainage holes in 2-inch-wide terra-cotta pots by scraping them with a drill bit. One by one, remove bulbs, and slip each light fixture through the drainage hole. Replace the bulbs, and hang the lights. Vary the theme with shades made from aluminum foil cupcake holders, tiny baskets, or … be inventive!

finishing touches: lighting

luxurious lighting

Illumination enhances a garden room's usefulness after the sun sets. Electric outdoor lighting converts dark spaces and shadowy corners into inviting living areas. What's more, night lighting promotes surefooting as well as your home's security.

If you make safety and security your lighting goals, tuck various kinds of lights beside paths, into stair-step risers, and near outdoor seating. Select strong-beam bulbs to discourage intruders.

To cast a welcoming glow, choose low-voltage lights to bathe an entry area with gentle illumination. Look for easy-to-install, low-voltage lighting kits at home centers, hardware stores, or on the Internet. Install light-sensitive, photocell timers to switch lights on and off automatically at dusk and dawn. Instead of lighting all areas of your garden uniformly, use a variety of fixtures with different angles of light, such as dramatic uplighting and traditional downlighting. Arrange illumination to create patches of light and darkness. Plan your lighting for easy lightbulb changing. Install a switch in the house for convenient control of landscape lights.

night lights

right and *far right:* Choose functional and beautiful light fixtures, repeating the style throughout your landscape. For a dramatic effect, use strands of lights to outline a structure, such as a gazebo, pergola, or arbor. Ceiling lights brighten this gazebo's interior.

installing low-voltage lights

1 lay the course Choose a low-voltage (typically 12-volt) lighting kit for economy, practicality, and ease of installation. Map the lighting route on paper; determine where you'll place the lamps. Following the manufacturer's directions, install the transformer (power) box on an outside wall near an outlet. Attach the low-voltage cable to the terminal screws on the transformer. Unwind the cable and lay it along the course for the lights.

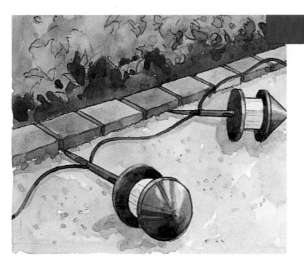

2 complete the connections Position light fixtures along the length of cable. Snap the fixtures onto the cable. With most lighting kits, teeth in each fixture's connector pierce the cable to create the electrical connection. Attach anchoring stakes to fixtures. Plug the transformer into the outlet to survey light placement. Make any necessary adjustments, then spike fixtures into the ground. Vary lamp heights as desired. A higher position expands the cast of light; a lower position reduces it.

3 position the lights When you're satisfied with the height and position of your lights, bury the cable 2 to 4 inches deep (unless code requirements specify otherwise). To bury the cable, slit the turf with a spade, lift the sod, lay the cable underneath, and replace the sod. In planting beds or paths, cover the cable with mulch, bark, or gravel. For a hands-free switch that automatically turns lights on and off, choose a light-sensitive transformer or install an outdoor timer.

finishing touches: accessories

details, details

Give your garden room that lived-in look by sprucing up the space with decorative touches. Combine items that reflect your personality and offer comfort. Trim your garden escape with a blend of favorite things, such as sculpture, furniture, and architectural salvage pieces. Save money by using pieces you have on hand. For a cohesive look, choose accessories with an overall motif or color scheme.

A courtyard (*shown right* and *opposite*) comes to life courtesy of carefully positioned cedar lattice screens.

artful mix

right: Coordinate an outdoor room with accessories that link their color or material. Aqua unifies this setting, from the wicker chair to the candlesticks, while the cedar bench and lattice work together.

Use lattice to divide an expansive yard into cozy getaways. Cut windows into lattice to open up vistas between rooms. If lattice isn't the look you want, consider bamboo screen, metal trellising, or rustic bentwood dividers. Substitute the wooden bench with a stylish cushioned chaise or wood-look rockers made from easy-care recycled plastic.

Although elements of style abound, the key to injecting personality into your garden rooms comes via planning and sticking to a theme. Color unifies and adds character with as much ease and boldness as a coat of exterior-grade paint or stain.

Tile also tops the list of decorative materials that bring color and personality to decorative accents. Choose weather-worthy tile to cover tables and floors and to trim walls. Explore a vast selection of ceramic, stone, glass, and other tile options in a wide range of sizes, from tiny mosaic pieces to generous steppers.

Find inspiration for decor themes in other materials as well. For instance, galvanized metal weaves a sophisticated theme in corrugated roofing or siding, planter boxes, garden stakes or signage, and a collection of watering cans, buckets, and washtubs. Stone, bamboo, terra-cotta, glass, wrought iron, and other materials offer endless decorating possibilities.

Keep in mind that decorating is an ongoing process; it's okay to change things that don't work.

circles and squares

left: Details turn an ordinary lattice screen into a compelling scene. Glass orbs and water plants fill a huge, old mixing bowl. A grapevine wreath encircles a square window.

garden rooms | **91**

garden-view bench

cost	make it	skill
$$$	weekend	easy

you will need

- two 4×8-foot pressure-treated or cedar lattice panels
- old coffee table top or ¾-inch plywood
- concrete pier footings
- four 4×4 posts (10 feet long)
- galvanized nails
- drill, jigsaw, circular saw
- galvanized deck screws
- two 2×4s (2 feet long), two 2×4s (3 feet long), two 2×4s (23¼ inches long), one 2×4 (26 inches long)
- leaded-glass window (optional), bolts
- three 1×4s (17 inches long), one 1×4 (29 inches long)
- two 1×6s (29 inches long)
- 2×2s (24 feet total)

bench beauty

right: Entwined with an overachieving clematis, this cozy trellis bench teams lattice (for architectural appeal) with an old leaded-glass window (for a touch of style). Weather-worthy cushions complete a comfy seat.

trellis retreat

Use your imagination to craft custom garden seating that does more than feel good. Combine stylish architectural elements to create a bench that's also a small sanctuary. Enclosing a bench with latticework panels provides a spot for intimate conversation or personal reflection, while giving vines a place to climb.

Prefabricated lattice provides a versatile, inexpensive option for adding architectural interest, trellising, or screening to a garden room. Cut lattice carefully; power saws can splinter strips and loosen nails. Brace lattice prior to sawing by tacking a 2×2 across the length of the panel at the halfway point. Lattice provides the

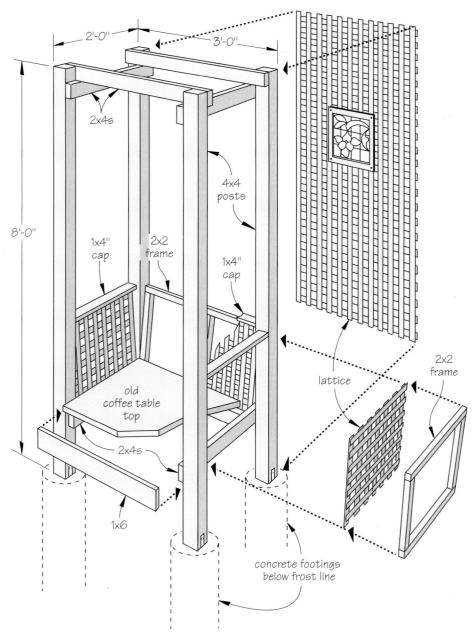

2'-0"

3'-0"

2x4s

4x4
posts

8'-0"

1x4"
cap

2x2
frame

1x4"
cap

old
coffee table
top

2x4s

1x6

lattice

2x2
frame

concrete footings
below frost line

right touch for wrapping a seat in secluded privacy. This trellis bench was built for about $150. An old coffee tabletop forms the seat (or substitute with ¾-inch plywood).

build the bench

You may want to add design flair by cutting a square or rectangular hole in the lattice and installing an old leaded-glass window.

Dig post holes to a depth that meets local requirements. Pour concrete footings and place post brackets in the top while the concrete is wet or place pre-made piers on the top of the footings. Attach the posts to the brackets with screws.

Nail two 2×4s inside the uprights to form the sides of the seat base and one 2×4 at the back between these two pieces to form the rear seat base. Nail upper 2×4s in place. Cut out a spot for the window in the back lattice panel. Attach the lattice to the outside back of the uprights. Drill four holes in the window-frame corners and bolt the window (optional) to the lattice.

Determine a comfortable height for the angled bench back. Make a T-shape brace of 2×2s, using screws to secure the T's horizontal piece to the insides of the back uprights. Attach the T's vertical piece to the center bottom of the rear seat base. Nail the lattice for the bench back to the seat base and to the T brace.

Build a 2×2 frame to support side lattice panels, which run from the base of the bench to the top of the frame. Attach the frame to insides of the front and back uprights; trim and attach the lattice to the frame. Attach arm and back support caps (1×4s), and the front and back bottom supports (1×6s). Nail 2×4s around the inside perimeter of the trellis top to stabilize the structure.

Consult our Home Improvement Encyclopedia for great do-it-yourself home repair projects at **www.bhg.com/bkhomeimprovement**

the
rooms

tour the rooms

Just as you gather ideas from a garden tour, find inspiration in the gamut of garden rooms on the following pages. Room by room, page by page, discover building techniques, decorative details, and creative approaches to carving an expanse of yard into a garden escape.

simplistic style Some rooms come into being by virtue of a landscape's existing attributes, such as a low-spreading tree, an ordinary shed or fence, a long-standing vine-cloaked arbor, or a simple patio or deck. Each of these features anchors a scene that, with basic embellishments, becomes a beautiful oasis. In the photo *opposite*, an existing hedge, layers of shrubs, and a circular planting bed define a lovely garden. But the bench adds stylish seating, while an added statue and ornamental planter outfit the room with appeal and personality.

form and function Think about how you want to use your outdoor spaces. Do you hanker for a haven to pass weekend afternoons in leisure? Do you seek a quiet, private alcove where you can light candles and relax? Do you want an outdoor dining room for everyday use and for entertaining, complete with furniture, cooking surfaces, a refrigerator, and a sink? With careful orchestration, you can design rooms around a specific use or for multiple purposes. Aim to arrange a traditional indoor/outdoor room, such as a family room, furnished porch, or garden hideaway with basic amenities: seating, lighting, and storage. Or gear up to create a 21st-century retreat: an outdoor office with Internet access, a bathing room with a whirlpool tub, or alfresco sleeping quarters with fully powered reading lamps and quiet music.

under cover Give your shelter panache by emphasizing details. Trade run-of-the-mill plastic chairs and a table for a comfortable ensemble with weather-resistant cushions. Tuck a sofa bed into a screen porch to rig a space that's perfect for after-work relaxing or pajama parties. Surround a deck with fast-growing ornamental grasses to form privacy walls that change with the seasons. Tailor a gazebo to double as a dining room or a spare bedroom. Imagine the possibilities!

natural environments

secret garden

Peaceful ambience abounds in a room that's shingled with vines and flowers. To construct your own rustic, tranquil retreat, start by choosing a place where plants form either a lush ceiling or verdant walls and a floor.

If you have only open space or lawn, create the illusion of a secret garden that seems to have been carved from woodland. Frame lattice walls and train vines to scramble across a ceiling of lattice or strands of steel wire strung in a grid. Romance blooms in a hideaway (*right*) with a mantle of trumpet vines (*Campsis radicans*) and grapevines. The vines require occasional trimming to prevent a too-wild look.

Underfoot, spread a weather-resistant surface on top of heavy-duty landscape fabric. Gravel, shredded-bark mulch, or coarse sand provide loose floorings that work hard for little installation effort, although all three prove cumbersome for moving furniture. Replace turf with soft groundcovers, such as Corsican mint or wooly thyme, in a semishaded area.

Outfit your room with comforts of home: lighting, furnishings, and fabrics. To keep with the natural theme, opt for accessories such as candles tucked into the hollows of rocks or tiki torches. Choose table linens made of woven reeds or leaf-print fabrics. Provide quirky seating, such as tree trunks, moss-covered chairs, or massive smooth stones. Plant a grassy welcome mat.

penchant for privacy

right: A leafy canopy adorns a lattice-framed structure. The cool cave seems to have sprouted from the ground. Always-open shutter doors and candlelight extend a cozy, friendly welcome.

earthy niches

Most gardens afford plenty of natural elements that serendipitously form perfect nooks for seclusion.

- Screens of any sort, including a hedge, an arbor, or an oversized shrub, create wonderful privacy walls. Use one of these elements as a starting point, if you wish, and build from there.

- A spreading tree casts an overhead canopy that effectively caps a room. Consider pruning the lower branches of a mature evergreen to shape an aromatic bower. Pine needles make a soft floor.

- A tree house is a dreamy escape for kids of all ages. Check local ordinances before building and ensure adequate support for the structure.

enchanted evenings
left: Entertain family and friends in your garden getaway by relying on lighting that's as natural as the room itself. Be safety conscious by keeping a fire extinguisher handy.

natural environments

planter's palette

Where a natural bower does not exist, purposefully placed plants build the framework for a garden room as surely as walls and other structural elements. If you plan to enjoy your garden room mostly in the morning, choose plants that will greet you and the day with fragrance, such as nicotiana, roses, and honeysuckle. Surround an evening-oriented place with sweet-scented hostas.

A shade-casting tree with low-hanging branches plays center stage in a garden room, easily sheltering seating and dining areas. A weeping tree also fills the role of sculptural focal point. Ornamental grasses accomplish many tasks in rooms, from shaping living walls to edging flower beds to anchoring an entry garden. Shrubs boast unsurpassed versatility, from groundcover to border; from hedge to focal point.

Plants also enhance the style of a garden space. A tightly clipped knot garden (*right*) dresses a room with the formality of a tuxedo. Conversely, the floriferous abandon of a fragrant climbing rose trained on a rustic arbor injects casual charm into a garden nook. Where trees or shrubs form a hidden corner, a secret garden lurks. Tucking a bench or a couple of chairs under a leafy bower provides a cool retreat on sweltering days.

Use hedges or mixed-shrub borders to create living walls. Select plants based on the look and maintenance level you desire. A formal hedge,

just a juxtaposition
right: **Charm aplenty results from juxtaposing formal and rustic elements. A classic knot garden woven from a boxwood hedge contrasts with an earthy arbor smothered with roses. A duet of urns bridges the gap between the styles.**

whether planted as a green work of art (*left*) or a living fence, requires regular trimming. Good plant choices for a tidy hedge include convex holly, wall germander, boxwood, arborvitae, and bay. In a shrub border, plants grow freely. Prune selectively to maintain shrub height and vigor. Make a shrub tapestry, rich in colors and textures, by planting Japanese quince, peonies, barberry, hydrangea, dwarf euonymus, juniper, and Shrub roses. Evergreen plants form year-round structure; deciduous plants provide views that change with the seasons. Include both coniferous and broadleaf evergreens for interesting diversity.

natural environments

easy does it

Having lots of space is not a prerequisite for creating a garden room. Equip rooms with only the bare necessities and you'll discover that enjoyment reigns supreme. Gather a few comfortable chairs beneath a spreading tree or tuck a bench into a shrub-protected corner. String a hammock between two sturdy trees. Forming a room is that simple.

Survey your existing outdoor spaces, looking for naturally screened areas. Remember that an overhead canopy, such as a tree, defines a room every bit as strongly as a lengthy hedge. Garden beds brimming with flowers also stage a natural backdrop for a seating area. Add furnishings that accommodate the way you intend to use the room.

sweet dreams

above right: **A hammock hung between two trees forms a space private enough for catching a few winks or catching up on a favorite book.**

meadow mystique

right: **Add cushions to cozy Adirondack chairs to increase the comfort level. These seats' wide arms provide perfect perches for drinks and snacks.**

A bench or swing suits intimate conversations; a table or teacart works for serving food or drinks.

Use your room in ways that expand your original intentions. For instance, if you arrange a table and chairs for enjoying leisurely meals outdoors, use the place as a fresh-air office or a game room for the kids. As you spend time in the room, you'll incorporate decorative elements that complement the space and make it more comfortable, useful, and alluring.

bistro bliss

left: When space is at a premium, count on a petite bistro set to meet seating and food serving needs. Place tables and chairs on a surface other than turf. Otherwise, you'll need to move the furniture with each mowing.

patios

concrete cover-up

Dress up a dull concrete patio by applying colorful stains that transform industrial gray into a stylish look. Easy, quick, and inexpensive, concrete stains dress up humdrum patio slabs, pool surrounds, walkways, block retaining walls, and garage floors.

Select concrete stain from a palette of muted hues, including green, yellow, brown, red, and blue. Precut stencils, available from most concrete stain manufacturers, enable you to create a custom look easily. Best of all, producing your own wall-to-wall artwork using concrete stains won't break your budget. Most stains cost less than $30 a gallon (1 gallon covers about 150 to 200 square feet).

Stains work like permanent marking pens. They bond with the concrete or other surface, leaving a lasting uniform color that, unlike paint, won't flake, fade, or crack over time. Water-base stains perform outdoors or indoors, on concrete, asphalt, and bare or previously painted surfaces. Solvent-base stains cannot be used on asphalt but work on unpainted outdoor surfaces.

You don't need mint-condition concrete to apply a stain to it. Cracks sometimes enhance color, giving it a weathered look. Allow new concrete to cure 30 to 45 days before applying stain. Although a waterproofing exterior sealer is not necessary, you may want to apply it in heavy-traffic areas. Once you apply a stain, the surface is walkable in 1 hour, but wait 72 hours before driving on it.

wall-to-wall color

right: **A formerly mildewed patio dons the look of modern art with shapely shades of concrete stain. The earthy yellow, green, and tan tones complement the color scheme of the adjacent indoor room.**

stunning stain

left: No longer a drab slab, this color-stained patio bubbles with personality. With a simple design, it's a do-it-yourself job. If your design entails elaborate details and more than a quartet of colors, consider hiring a professional.

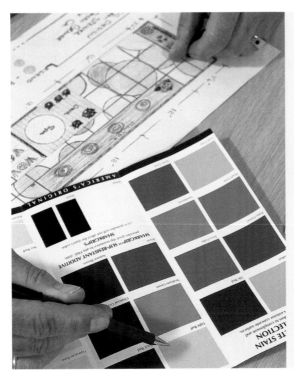

color selection

Measure your concrete area and draw it to scale on paper. Sketch a design using simple geometric shapes. You'll eventually pencil the pattern onto the concrete, so keep figures simple enough for rendering onto slab. When selecting colors, focus on established schemes in surrounding plantings as well as outdoor furnishings and fabrics. Match the house trim or indoor rooms that open onto the patio. Plan hues carefully, making final selections outdoors in natural light where you plan to stain. Remember that colors sometimes appear darker or more intense when spread over a large area. Experiment with each color in an unobtrusive area before applying it to a sizable concrete section.

patios

1   **clean** To stain a concrete slab, first sweep the patio to remove loose dirt and debris. Spray the surface using a garden hose outfitted with a pressure nozzle. Protect surrounding plantings with a plastic tarp. Secure the tarp around the edges of the concrete to prevent chemicals from seeping into nearby soil. Remove oil with a degreasing solution. Allow the degreaser to sit for 5 minutes. Wearing waterproof gloves, scrub the area using a stiff brush. Rinse the scrubbed section. Work in 10×10-foot sections so the degreaser doesn't dry before you rinse it. Let the concrete dry.

2   **bleach** Brush any areas tinged with algae or mildew using a solution of half water, half household bleach. Wearing a mask and gloves, apply the solution and scrub until the algae or mildew is gone. Rinse the area thoroughly using a garden hose to wash away any bleach residue. Allow the concrete to dry.

3   **etch** Open the pores in the concrete to accept the color stain by etching the surface. In a plastic watering can, mix 1 part etcher to 2 parts water. Pour the solution onto the concrete, and agitate it using a stiff broom until foaming stops. Work in small sections to prevent the solution from drying before rinsing. To rinse, scrub with a brush while applying water; work in sections. Wipe the area using clean rags. If residue appears, rinse again. Let the concrete dry for 24 hours.

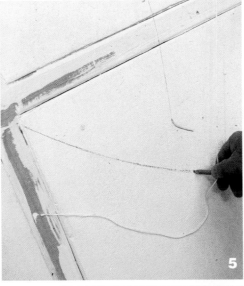

stain Sweep the patio clean. Stain the **4**
entire surface with your background color.
Brush or roll on a heavy first coat of stain,
applying it in one direction. Allow the stain
to dry. Brush or roll on a second coat,
applying it in the opposite direction. After
the second coat dries, inspect the color
and coverage to determine if a third coat
is needed. If so, apply it diagonally or
in a direction that crisscrosses the other
two applications. Water-base stains dry in
approximately 2 hours; solvent-base stains
require 12 hours.

sketch Choose or create a design. **5**
Mimic a pattern from your home, repeat
a tilelike pattern, make a border around
the patio's edge, cover the area with a rug
image, or stain a star in the center of the
area. Transfer your design onto the concrete
using chalk or a pencil. Make heavy-paper
stencils (to scale), if you prefer, to ensure
replication of a precise pattern. Otherwise,
a straightedge helps you draw lines exactly;
a string tied to the chalk or pencil forms a
compass for drawing circles and curves. Use
masking tape to outline design areas, making
crisp lines to protect edges of areas you don't
want stained.

color Using a brush or roller, stain **6**
each part of your design. Follow the same
procedure as with the base coats. Save and
reuse excess stain (use it to color concrete
stepping-stones or furniture). If you wish,
apply a clear concrete sealer to protect the
finished surface.

millstone fountain

cost	make it	skill
$$$	weekend	moderate

you will need

- shovel
- plastic tub (5-foot diameter, 18 inches deep)
- ready-mix concrete
- small submersible pump
- 28-inch-long plastic tube
- 6-inch-diameter perforated PVC pipe (22 inches long)
- three or four 6-inch-diameter PVC pipes (25 inches long)
- round river rock (1½- to 4-inch size)
- millstone (4-foot diameter), or large flat rock

makeover magic

What to do with a small, flat, and poorly draining site where grass struggles to grow? Compose a stylish garden room with a bluestone patio, woodland plantings that covet moist roots, and a millstone fountain gently spouting water.

This ground, now a room (*opposite*), supported a garage and driveway for 60 years. When these elements were removed and the soil was exposed, the yard became a mucky swamp. Adding sand and organic matter to the soil improved its drainage and fertility, but it took more than a few plantings to create a garden escape. A beautiful stone floor and comfortably functional table and chairs outfitted the room in purposeful style, but a focal point remained elusive. A millstone fountain solved the problem, adding instant drama and delight to the simple scene.

fountain artistry

right: **A millstone-turned-fountain provides the focal point for a garden room. River rocks decorate the surface and perimeter of the fountain. It's also an ideal place for the rocks gathered on hikes or vacations.**

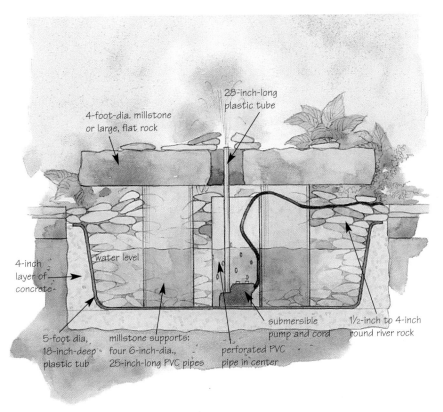

4-foot-dia. millstone or large, flat rock

28-inch-long plastic tube

4-inch layer of concrete

water level

5-foot dia, 18-inch-deep plastic tub

millstone supports: four 6-inch-dia., 25-inch-long PVC pipes

perforated PVC pipe in center

submersible pump and cord

1½-inch to 4-inch round river rock

Constructing a millstone fountain requires no special skills. Finding an authentic millstone (historically used for grinding grain) can be tricky. Alternatively, achieve the same effect by drilling a 4-inch-diameter hole in the center of a large flat rock. Or drill a hole in the bottom of a big, low ceramic bowl to accommodate the fountain jet.

Prepare to install a millstone fountain by siting it near an outlet equipped with a ground fault circuit interrupter (GFCI); install a GFCI outlet if one doesn't exist. Excavate a hole to hold the plastic tub (water reservoir). Line the hole with a 4-inch-thick layer of ready-made concrete for a sturdy base for the fountain. After several days, when the concrete has dried, insert the tub. The tub should sit level and flush with the ground. Add or remove soil until the area is level with the top edge of the tub.

Attach a fountain jet to a small submersible pump. Position the assembly inside the perforated PVC pipe. Stand the pipe and pump on the bottom of the tub. Set up the remaining PVC pipes to support the millstone. Fill in around these pipes with layers of round river rock, until the rocks are within an inch of the tops of the millstone support pipes. Fill the reservoir with water and connect the pump to your home's electrical source. Adjust the water flow of the pump to create the amount of bubble or spray desired. With strong helpers, position the millstone over the fountain jet. Top the stone and surround its perimeter with river rocks. Add water to the reservoir periodically to offset evaporation, especially during hot weather.

natural feel
left: **The natural tones of a bluestone patio blend beautifully with surrounding plantings; the enticing setting entails little upkeep. The fountain imitates a bubbling woodland spring.**

patios

problem solvers

Carving living space from a yard that's too small, too exposed, or too hilly is a challenge. But it also is an avenue for creativity. No matter how difficult your yard seems, adding a patio instantly opens up a realm of outdoor living possibilities.

Overcome a compact or narrow yard by slicing the space into smaller garden areas *(below right)*. Use different flooring materials, such as brick, turf, and gravel, to outline the areas. and achieve a sense of spacious luxury. Add lush plantings to suggest an atmosphere of abundance.

If neighboring properties rub shoulders with yours, boost privacy with structural elements that establish seclusion, frame views, and provide more space for growing plants. A pergola offers shelter from glaring sun and blocks views from upper floors of nearby homes. Add a peristyle *(opposite top)*, a curving

architectural art
above: Add the curve and columns of a classic peristyle to open a small space, frame a view, and define an intimate room.

dynamic duo
right: A confined yard blooms into two spacious garden rooms, thanks to distinctive flooring and a transition area between the two rooms. Plantings direct views and traffic flow, overcoming the boxiness of the space.

structure borrowed from Greek architecture, to screen views. The elegant structure also creates an illusion of depth that makes a small area appear larger. Wrap columns with climbing roses, which will cover the entire structure with easy beauty. Other good plant choices include wisteria, bittersweet, clematis, or Carolina jessamine.

downhill trickle

left: **Put a slope to work as a natural bed for a tumbling waterfall and stream. Place a brick-floor seating area at one end of the water feature; edge it with wet-loving plants.**

plan the perfect patio

You're more likely to use a garden room if it includes the elements you desire most. But you may not have identified those yet. Use these tips to determine what you want and how to get it:

- **dream a little:** Before you tear out that old patio or build a new one, think about how you want to use the space. If you plan to entertain, how many people could the area accommodate? Do you want the room to be open to the stars, drenched in sun, or protected from both?

- **take another look:** What do you see when you look at the patio area (existing or potential) from various rooms in the house? How could you improve the view year-round?

- **think outside the box:** If you have a sloping yard, put gravity to work and turn it into a trickling water feature. Include a small terrace with a seating area at the top of the watercourse. Plan a patio at the base of the stream and enjoy the full effect of the scene.

- **move it:** If you plan to acquire furniture for your outdoor room, consider pieces that could move indoors for off-season use.

decks: pergola topper

cost	make it	skill
$$$	4 days	moderate

you will need

eight 4×4 posts

concrete premix

two 4×8 side beams
(20 feet, 6 inches
long)

fourteen 4×4
truss tops
(6 feet, 9 inches long);
twenty−one 4×4s
(short truss pieces);
seven 4×4 truss
bottoms (9 feet long)

4×8 ridge beam
(20 feet, 6 inches long)

galvanized deck
screws

compound miter
saw, drill

open-air room

Count on a deck to extend the comforts of your home past its walls. Customize the structure by adding architectural details, such as curved edges, multiple levels, or overhead beams.

Include gravity-defying furniture, such as hanging chairs, a swing, or a hammock. Add overhead support to suspend these footloose seats. Settle on a structural design that echoes the architectural elements of your house. Repeat rooflines, for instance.

This fresh-air family room (right) features a double-decker floor plan with a pergola, a boardwalk, and swinging chairs. To build this pergola, use pressure-treated wood for frames and posts; choose cedar for the other parts. Join all pieces with galvanized deck screws. Paint or stain the wood before constructing the pergola.

Dig postholes to just below the frost line. Insert the 4×4 posts and fill the holes with concrete. (Read about setting a post on page 51.)

double-layer decking

right: **A deck that adjoins a home through wide-access doors extends indoor living spaces with impressive square footage.**

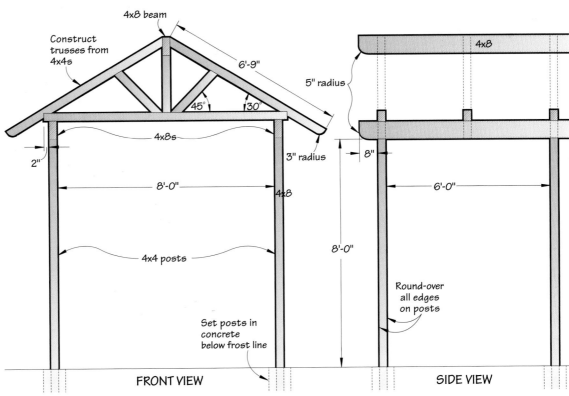

Construct trusses from 4x4s

4x8 beam

6'-9"

45° 30°

4x8s

5" radius

3" radius

4x8

2"

8'-0"

4x4 posts

Set posts in concrete below frost line

FRONT VIEW

4x8

8"

6'-0"

8'-0"

Round-over all edges on posts

SIDE VIEW

Attach the two 4x8 side beams to the tops of the posts. Prebuild two trusses (from 4x4s) and have a friend help you mount one at the front and one at the rear of the structure, using galvanized deck screws. Then carefully lift the 4x8 ridge beam into place and screw the two trusses to it. Either prebuild the remaining five trusses and install each as a complete unit, or assemble them in place, one piece at a time.

If you wish, hang the chairs from the ridge beam, using eyebolts and swivel hooks.

deck extension

left: A boardwalk topped with a pergola extends the deck into the garden. Hanging chairs provide breezy alternative seating to the formal furnishings in the outdoor family room on the deck.

garden rooms | **113**

decks: stained rug

cost	make it	skill
$$	weekend	easy

you will need

- deck cleaner and stiff brush
- tape measure
- T square and chalk line
- utility knife
- exterior-grade wood stain
- tapered bristle brush
- disposable sponge applicator

wooden retreat

Dress up the bare-board floors and railings of a deck with clever touches of color and creativity. Vintage porch molding brings ornate charm to the scene (*right*). Finials attached beneath house eaves, upside down spandrels screwed atop deck rails, and salvage boards nailed to built-in seating suggest the look of an old-fashioned porch and add privacy. Large containers overflow with fast-growing annuals, forming a living screen.

Underfoot, a dull deck gives way to a custom area rug created with exterior stain. To make a similar floor, use an old bedsheet to help visualize the rug's size and shape; then on graph paper sketch to scale designs that suit your decorating strategy. A checkerboard pattern fits the cottage style of this haven. For a more formal look, try a double-bordered solid rug. Go for whimsy with curlicues and circles. Make a rug with hand (and paw) prints of family and friends.

magic carpet

right: Roll out a colorful deck rug, courtesy of wood stain. A festive checkerboard design, made with two shades of exterior stain, transforms ordinary pressure-treated pine into a fanciful surface. Vintage wood details and window shutters assume new roles as deck railing and privacy screens. Bent willow furnishings complete the fashionable retreat.

1 clean and draw Clean the wood using a deck cleaner and a stiff brush. Use a T square and chalk line to mark out the rug design. As you mark lines, step back and see if they appear straight or have someone help you ensure the lines are straight. Create stencils for intricate designs and trace them with chalk. The checkerboard rug is a 93-inch square composed of 15-inch squares framed by a 9-inch-wide border.

2 score and stain Score ¼-inch-deep design lines using a utility knife to prevent the stain from bleeding into adjacent areas. Scoring creates a thin well in which runoff stain will pool. Begin staining with the lightest color stain. Work your way from the center of the rug outward. Stain every other square, using a tapered bristle brush; a disposable sponge applicator makes straight edges. Let the stain dry completely, according to the manufacturer's directions. Fill in the remaining squares with a darker shade. Stain the border last.

knock on wood
Search for vintage woodwork trims at demolition sites, salvage yards, auctions, and antique shops. Check for rot by pricking the wood with a penknife. Soft, spongy spots indicate a problem. Plan to remove and repair small rot patches with wood filler. Inspect bottom edges for warping. If warping won't affect your project, purchase the piece. New, machine-milled pine trim is affordable and develops a vintage look as it weathers.

decks

free agents

When the scenery boasts beauty that begs for
seating positioned to take in the view, opt for a
freestanding deck. Construct it anywhere that a
patio would fit. Also choose decking to conquer
problem areas. A deck tames a slope like nothing
else, providing living space in an unused area.
Terrace a deck along a hillside, perching it atop the
peak or tucking it into a steep grade. Provide access
with sturdy paths that are easy on your feet, such
as large stepping-stones or more decking.

Your deck may need railings. For most
communities, building codes require railings on
decks that stand more than 30 inches off the
ground. Check local ordinances to be sure your
deck meets the code. If you can, leave the sides
railing-free and nestle plantings along the deck's
edge to make deck and surroundings one. Or edge
the platform with benches instead of railings.

Add details, such as lighting or outdoor
speakers, depending on how you intend to use
the space. If you enjoy grilling and your deck is
situated near the house, consider running a gas
line to the outdoor room for greater ease in fueling
your grill without the hassles of bottled gas.

showstopping scenery
right: **A freestanding deck with comfortable
chairs and a great vista becomes a favorite
place to gather with family and friends. Position
the deck so you can enjoy the view every day.
Add a table for dining, especially if your view
includes sunrises or sunsets.**

decked out

left: Decorate a spacious freestanding deck with container gardens, wind art, or statuary. Include a tabletop fountain to add the soothing sound of running water.

decorative strategy

Furnish a freestanding deck with ensembles that suit the scene. A simple park-style bench affords ample seating. Provide a market umbrella if there are no trees to cast cooling shade. For an area you use infrequently, select sturdy metal or weather-resistant wooden seating. If your deck represents an outdoor family room, stock it with cushioned chairs and chaises. Include a table for eating and end tables to hold drinks. A coffee table encircled with a bench and chairs encourages conversation. If heavy winds sweep regularly across your deck, choose furniture that's weighty enough to withstand the blasts, or you'll be chasing chairs and tables across your yard. Built-in seating won't go astray. Consider using it for a deck positioned to capture views in a far-flung reach of your yard or to provide additional seating if you frequently entertain large numbers of guests.

courtyards

walled gardens

A courtyard forms the quintessential garden room, blurring the lines between indoors and outdoors. The distinguishing feature of a courtyard lies in what surrounds it: walls. Whether literal walls or other forms, such as vine-covered fences, hedges, espalier, or latticework screens, walls define and enclose a courtyard.

Sophisticated modern courtyards afford a secluded place stocked with plants, a comfortable place to rest, and a water feature. When designing and decorating a courtyard, scale affects each decision. In a typically small area, the presence of walls necessitates trim furnishings that fit the enclosed space. Metal, wood, or rattan furniture with slender profiles would suit a confined garden niche.

Select plants that enrich the area with artistic character, such as textural foliage,

unusual flowers, or heavy fragrance. If planting beds won't work into the landscape plan, use container gardens to enliven the space. Use fewer, larger containers, including a few exquisitely ornamental pots that brim with simple plantings, such as rye grass, an upright ornamental grass, or a trim dwarf conifer.

When a hedge frames a courtyard, trim shrubs at the appropriate time of year. Shape the hedge, making the top narrower than the bottom, enabling sunlight to reach all growing points. In regions with heavy snowfall, round the top of the hedge to shed snow.

formal foyer

left: **Strikingly simple plantings, arranged around a central axis, make a bold first impression in a front courtyard that buffers the home from street noise. Neatly clipped boxwood hedges border planting beds. Annuals march through the seasons in colorful ranks. The living fence of cherry laurel surrounds the courtyard and defines the space.**

courtyards

walled sanctuaries

Design a courtyard to transform a problematic part of your landscape into a choice room. Terraced and rimmed with retaining walls (*right*), a steep neglected space next to the house provides a place to garden and savor privacy. The carefully orchestrated courtyard beckons with design features and thoughtfully chosen decorative details.

Because most courtyards snuggle between homes, their outlines feature boxy shapes and right angles. Play off that framework by making planting beds that reflect the shape of the space and by choosing paving materials that echo the look.

When designing a courtyard, consider the view into the area from all available angles. If the courtyard gives way to a lovely view, cut a window in a wall to frame it.

Include seating to make savoring the surroundings inviting and pleasant. Simple furniture styles suit a small space, as does a single-color scheme that's not overbearing. Pastel and earth-tone textiles blend into the background, but a bold hue splashed about sparingly among plantings and fixtures creates a delightful effect.

The more entries your courtyard offers, the more likely you are to use the space. If only one entry exists, keep it as open as possible to maneuver garden gear or furnishings through it. Include water and power sources inside your courtyard to maximize its decorative and utilitarian purposes.

cozy quarters
right: **A courtyard between house and street buffers noise and offers a serene setting for a garden stroll.**

courtyard essentials

- **simplicity:** Follow an overall plan. It saves time, money, and the frustration of a piecemeal installation. Choose shrubs and groundcovers for a green backdrop; add color with potted bloomers.

- **scale:** In a tight space, use small-scale materials and features, such as cobblestones instead of stepping-stone-size pavers, or an arbor instead of a gazebo.

- **beauty:** Create a view where none exists, using climbing plants, a water feature, or an artful structure. Disguise a storage area with a trellis and climbing plants. Paint faux scenery on a blank wall; picture an open-air marketplace, an ornate fountain, or the rolling hills of a distant landscape.

splish splash

above: A small, quiet fountain works well in a courtyard, where the sound of the splashing water tends to echo gently.

courtyards

indoor-outdoor rooms

No matter the climate, plan a courtyard to provide year-round enjoyment, offering a place to unwind and reconnect with nature. If possible, make the space easily accessible from the house. Where a courtyard provides an extension of the house, use similar design elements in both areas to smooth the transition from indoors to outdoors.

Increase the courtyard's apparent size by hanging mirrors on walls, adding a still pool to reflect the sky, or painting a scenic vista on a wall. Enliven the enclosed view by hanging framed pictures or tile mosaics and lanterns.

wall art

above: Build an artistic brick wall by incorporating windows. Twine vining plants through salvaged wrought-iron railing to soften the strong lines of the metalwork.

ups and downs

right: Changes in levels among plants, brick floors, and furnishings compose an easygoing rhythm. Vertical elements (small trees, a market umbrella, and vines) draw the eye upward.

Aim for beautiful and manageable plantings. The walls of a courtyard create microclimates that protect plants from wind and sun and may prevent rainfall from reaching soil. The confined environment may also increase the likelihood of growing plants not typically hardy in your region. A sheltered southern wall in Zone 5 could support plants normally found in Zones 6 or 7.

Plant compact trees and shrubs as the backbone for your small garden; select ones for year-round interest. Train vines on trellises and walls to conserve precious garden space. Choose flowering plants that exude luxurious fragrances, such as roses, sweet autumn clematis, moonflower, heliotrope, jasmine, or daphne.

aquatic delight
below: Incorporate a water feature into your courtyard. The sound of running water plays a relaxing lullaby that's easily appreciated in a tiny space and draws you outdoors.

rooftop room

sky-high sanctuary
Live large in the smallest yard by setting your sights high. Rooftop gardening opens a whole new arena for space-constrained gardeners. Rooms that give you a bird's-eye view of the ground promise privacy and afford as many planting areas as you would like.

Before building a rooftop garden room, consult with an architect or structural engineer for advice on how to reinforce existing structures to accommodate the additional weight of raised planting beds and decking. Plan to site heavy items, such as planters, near the edges of your skyscraping room. Choose lightweight materials, such as fiberglass, plastic, resin, and PVC for furniture, pots, and even decking materials. Include electrical outlets and water spigots in your rooftop room.

Lay deck planks over existing roofing. Screw instead of nail decking down to allow raising the deck for roof repairs. Enclose your room's perimeter with waist-high planters, built-in benches, or lattice walls. Lattice panels weigh less than a solid wall and let breezes blow through.

Plan your rooftop room with convenience and comfort in mind. Include easy access to your sky-high getaway, providing more than one entry/exit if possible. Build a small landing on a steep staircase to make the ascent and descent easier. Edge the landing deck with potted flowers for color.

Arrange comfortable furniture in your room, and add a canopy or an umbrella for protection from glaring sun or drenching rain.

high-rise garden
left: For gardeners with heavily shaded beds at ground level, a rooftop garden opens possibilities to grow sun-loving plants. Select drought-tolerant bloomers that stand up to wind and sun, such as marigold, coreopsis, calendula, golden marguerite, and sunflowers. Include a small tree, such as a Japanese maple in a pot. Incorporate water-retentive crystals into soil in planters to minimize watering chores.

pergola-covered rooms

made in the shade

When your yard contains little more than hot, dry space, create an inviting oasis of cooling shade and uncover many options for outdoor living. A simple pergola provides cover overhead; vines form a verdant canopy. Design a pergola with graceful columns to add structure and visual impact in your landscape. Create a look similar to this scene (*right*) by hiring a concrete contractor to pour concrete columns in large cardboard tubes (Sonatubes). When the tubes are cut away, they leave a circular swirl in the concrete. Choose to blend the lines, or leave them in place, using a sandblaster to give texture and an aged-looking finish to the columns.

Ask the concrete professional to set eye hooks in the tops of the columns for anchoring the pergola's steel-wire framework. Using heavy-duty wire,

form a taut framework from column to column. Weave wires into an overall grid.

Train perennial vines to climb the columns and grow over the grid. Plant wisteria, climbing roses, clematis, trumpet vine, ivy, climbing hydrangea, or akebia. Trim vines to keep them neat looking.

fired up

left: An elegant outdoor room replaces a plain backyard with a concrete terrace, a firebox, and a mosaic-embellished chimney. Concrete columns support a wisteria-draped pergola. The room proves inviting and cool in hot weather; cozy and comfortable when the weather turns chilly. An added grill rack turns the fireplace into a cooker.

garden rooms | **127**

cost	make it	skill
$$$	3 days	moderate

you will need

- shovel
- gravel or crushed rock
- four 6×6 posts
- quick-setting concrete
- nineteen 2×6s (12 feet long)
- eight 2×12s (12 feet long)
- four 1×12s (10 feet long)
- wood screws
- wood putty
- wood sealer (optional)
- exterior-grade primer and paint or stain (optional)

arched elegance

The open nature of a pergola lends a sense of luxurious spaciousness to a garden area that can't afford to be a fully enclosed room. Those space-constrained instances include rooms in front yards, narrow side yards, and tiny backyards. A pergola forms a room with clearly defined boundaries and unobstructed views. Most pergolas feature a roof of lattice weave or a grid of some sort. Celebrate outdoor living in grand style by constructing an arched roof that commands attention as an architectural feature and reflects the curving edges of nearby flower beds.

For inside the pergola, select flooring material that's durable and furniture-friendly. A bench or a pair of armchairs and a coffee table fit comfortably into this pergola. Choose weather-worthy fabrics when adding cushions. Mark the entrance to your pergola in formal style with a pair of globe-shape boxwood shrubs or matching topiaries.

private parlor

right: **Create a place for conversation or contemplation by tucking a bench beneath a round-top pergola. A brick-and-stone floor completes the scene.**

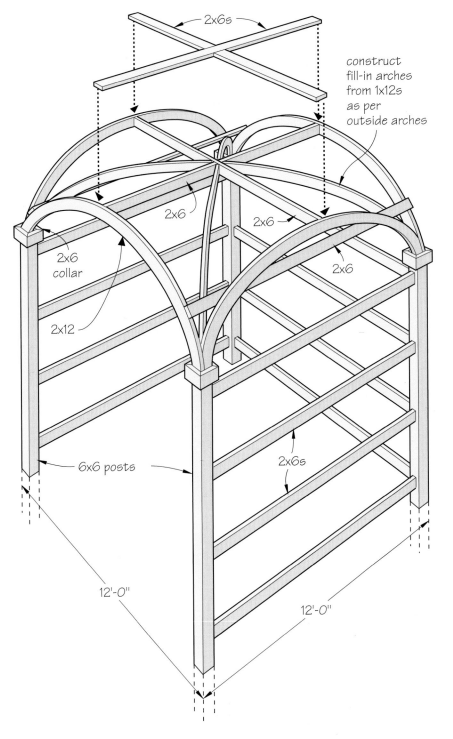

2x6s

construct
fill-in arches
from 1x12s
as per
outside arches

2x6

2x6

2x6
collar

2x6

2x12

6x6 posts

2x6s

12'-0"

12'-0"

build the arched pergola

Use the diagrams to construct a stylish pergola for your garden room. Adjust the dimensions and the materials to suit your space. Start with pressure-treated lumber or cedar for superior weatherability.

Set posts below the frost line. See page 51 for details. Trim ends from 2x6 crossbars to fit between posts; attach crossbars to posts using angled screws. Top posts with 2x6 collars. Construct the four outside arches from 2x12s using half-lap joints. Enlisting the help of a friend, position the arches atop the 2x6 post collars. Attach the 2x6 pieces to the arches as shown to stabilize them. Add the four fill-in arches. For a neat look, countersink all wood screws; then cover with wood putty. Apply a wood sealer to protect your structure and preserve the lumber's natural color; otherwise, let it weather. If you plan to stain or prime and paint your pergola, do so after construction.

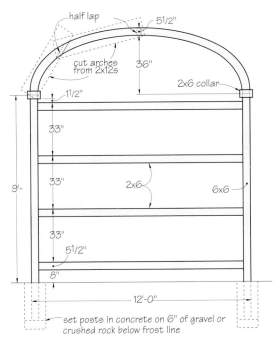

half lap

51/2"

cut arches
from 2x12s

36"

2x6 collar

11/2"

33"

9'-

33"

2x6

6x6

33"

51/2"

8"

12'-0"

set posts in concrete on 6" of gravel or
crushed rock below frost line

pergola-covered rooms: bamboo

cost	make it	skill
$$$	4 days	advanced

you will need

6×6s (upright posts, roof beams)

2×6s (decking, bench fronts, seats)

2×8s (joists, band joists, bench backs)

2×4s (roof slats, crossbars, bench and table frames, deck railings)

4×6s (roof crossbeams)

4×4s (deck-rail posts)

1×6s (tabletops)

2×2s (bench legs, tabletop spacers)

deck screws

½-inch wooden dowels

¾×1¾-inch trim

¾×2½-inch trim

1-inch plastic pipe

wire

bamboo-and-reed matting

backyard resort

Cultivate the look, feel, and appeal of a resort with a garden room that's decked out with serene ambience and comfort. The space devoted to a get-away-from-it-all setting need not be large. This 10×14-foot deck boasts big style without taking up the entire backyard.

In small rooms, rely on built-in furnishings to make the most of space. Keep railings low and open, to define the space without enclosing it. Designate areas for socializing or relaxing by arranging furniture appropriately. Leave an open area for children to play.

Building a breezy retreat (right) requires carpentry skills. Tackle the project in stages, starting with the deck, adding the pergola, and then completing deck railings, benches, and tabletops.

sunscreen on high

right: **A pergola covered in bamboo-and-reed matting screens the sun and withstands weather. Bamboo fares especially well in climates with freeze-thaw cycles. A thatched roof made with reed lasts for decades.**

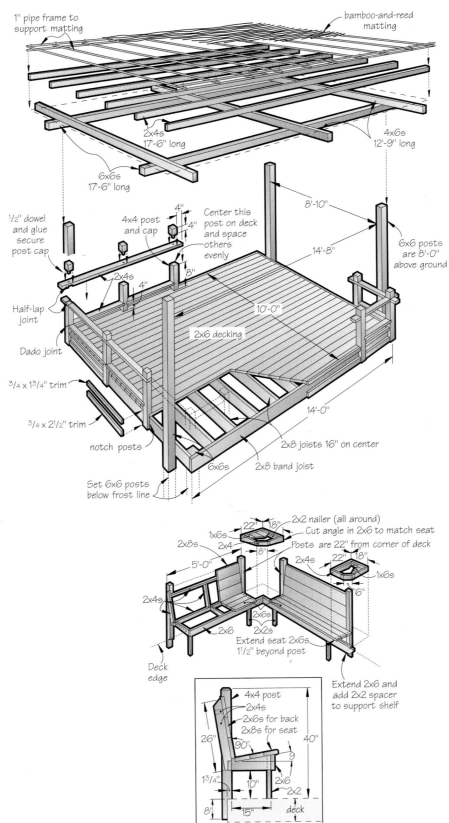

1" pipe frame to support matting

bamboo-and-reed matting

2x4s 17'-6" long

4x6s 12'-9" long

6x6s 17'-6" long

1/2" dowel and glue secure post cap

4x4 post and cap

Center this post on deck and space others evenly

4"
4"
4"
8"
4"

8'-10"

6x6 posts are 8'-0" above ground

14'-8"

2x4s

Half-lap joint

10'-0"

2x6 decking

Dado joint

3/4 x 1³/4" trim

3/4 x 2¹/2" trim

notch posts

6x6s

2x8 band joist

14'-0"

2x8 joists 16" on center

Set 6x6 posts below frost line

2x2 nailer (all around)

22" 18"

Cut angle in 2x6 to match seat

1x6s

2x8s

2x4

8"

Posts are 22" from corner of deck

5'-0"

22" 18"

2x4s

1x6s

2x4s

6"

2x6s

2x6

2x2s

Extend seat 2x6s 1¹/2" beyond post

Deck edge

Extend 2x6 and add 2x2 spacer to support shelf

4x4 post

2x4s

2x6s for back

2x8s for seat

26"

90°

40"

9

1³/4"

10"

2x6

2x2

8'

15"

deck

Enlist professionals to do all or part of the work if you prefer.

To begin, set posts in the ground below the frost line in your region. See page 51 for details. Build the deck, mounting the perimeter 2x8 band joists in place first and then adding the 2x8 joists. Use wood screws to hold decking in place. Screw the roof beams (6x6s and 4x6s) and crossbars (2x4s) in place. Use wire to assemble the pipe frame for the roof; attach it to the crossbars with nails driven through predrilled holes. Wire the bamboo-and-reed matting to the pipe frame. Build rails along the deck edges. Construct the benches and tabletops; attach them to the decking.

Purchase bamboo-and-reed matting or thatching from Internet or mail-order suppliers or from garden centers. Evaluate samples in terms of shade-casting ability and weatherability before selecting a roofing material.

pergola-covered rooms: basic

cost	make it	skill
$$	3 days	moderate

you will need

- four 6×6 posts (10 feet long)
- compound miter saw, drill
- eight 2×8 crossbeams (18 feet long)
- four 2×10 main beams (16 feet long)
- builder's square
- sixteen 9-inch carriage bolts
- eleven 2×4 rafters
- wood screws, lag screws
- shovel

hillside hideaway

Cope with a sloping site by perching a pergola atop it. The hillside landing supplies a level surface for a pergola furnished with a patio and roomy chairs.

Retaining walls buttress the stairs and provide a place to heap soil from the bank to form raised flower beds. Stairs master the steep grade with ease, occupying little space, and traversing the incline in a way that won't make it an arduous climb.

Plant a hillside with ground-hugging plants to control erosion and eliminate mowing. Traditional groundcovers, such as bugleweed, pachysandra, periwinkle, or hosta, quickly cover a bank with greenery. Vines also carpet slopes with color. Try ivy, clematis, honeysuckle, or Virginia creeper. Scotch broom, groundcover rose ('Flower Carpet'), Japanese juniper (*Juniperus procumbens*), and cotoneaster are shrubs that can handle hills. Plant densely to fill in the area within the first two growing seasons.

pergola retreat

right: **Tackle an incline by topping it with a pergola. Roses and wisteria surround the room with seasonal appeal.**

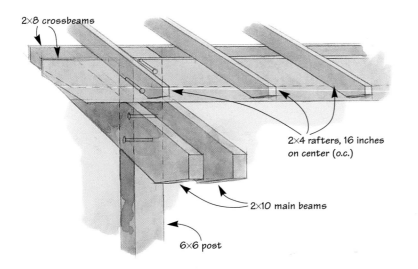

2×8 crossbeams

2×4 rafters, 16 inches
on center (o.c.)

2×10 main beams

6×6 post

build a basic pergola

No matter where you place a pergola (on a terraced slope, over a patio, or extending from the house), this 12×14-foot structure (*below left*) is a project that those with modest carpentry skills can tackle. Follow these plans and instructions to build a comparable pergola or customize them to suit your needs.

Set posts as described on page 51. Measure down 7¼ inches from the top of each post and mark a line indicating the top edge of each main beam. Then, with the aid of a friend, attach the four main beams (in pairs) to the posts, with one beam running along each side of the post. Insert carriage bolts through predrilled holes. Add the four pairs of crossbeams (2×8s). Bolt the two outside pairs of crossbeams to the posts in the same way you attached the main beams. Use wood screws, angled through the crossbeams into the main beams to hold the inner two pairs of beams in place. Finally, install the 11 rafters (2×4s) on top of the crossbeams, using 5-inch lag screws.

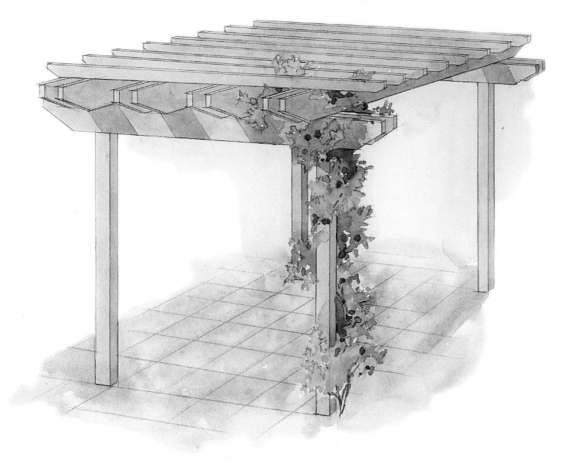

gazebo rooms: sleeping/dining

open-air oasis

A vine-covered gazebo blends family-friendly function into any backyard, no matter the size. The one shown *right* and *opposite* serves year-round outdoor living. It provides a family dining room or sleeps as many as six kids for a slumber party. The gazebo also serves as a meeting room. Design your gazebo to suit your garden lifestyle. Begin with a simple hexagonal shape set on concrete piers to lift the floor above ground level.

plush palace
above right: Lush morning glories cover the gazebo with living color.

fresh-air fare
right: Steps provide extra seating and ample space for container gardens.

weekend luxury

Dress your gazebo for outdoor dining during the week with a table and chairs, but on the weekend outfit it for leisurely living with a foam mattress cut to fit the floor dimensions. Upholster a 4-inch-thick round mattress with weather-worthy fabric and add sham-covered bed pillows. Enjoy your gazebo as a fresh-air family room with plenty of space for casual conversation, reading, and napping.

comfort zone

left: A foam mattress and plenty of throw pillows make a lounge-friendly family room. This 7½×7-foot redwood-and-cedar structure features stepped sides topped with a ledge that serves as a backrest and a place to set refreshments.

garden rooms | **135**

gazebo rooms: wrought iron

romantic retreat

Why travel to far-flung places when you can enjoy the experience of an intimate getaway by planning a patio retreat that overflows with classic appeal? A wrought-iron gazebo (*right*) assembles easily from a kit. It adorns a backyard with the look of a formal English structure and the feel of a romantic fantasy. The retreat took root on a boring concrete slab, transforming an abandoned patio into an outdoor destination.

Pea gravel spread on top of the concrete yields a new look without any digging, jackhammering, or staining. Redwood bender board secured by stakes keeps the gravel from spilling into the surrounding lawn. Wrought-iron and rattan furnishings equip the gazebo with the necessities for outdoor dining. Natural-hue serving pieces and linens transform everyday meals and snacks into special-occasion fare. Wrought-iron candleholders flank the gazebo's entryway.

Generous containers anchor the four corners of the gazebo with rounded lines that echo the curving wrought-iron structure. Tropical mandevilla vines twine up the gazebo's arched sides. In regions with harsh winters, plant hardy vines, such as climbing roses, trumpet vine, or wisteria, directly into the ground at the base of the gazebo. Use containers near the vines, filling them to overflowing with colorful annuals.

Washable mosquito netting drapes luxuriously over the 9½×7-foot-wide gazebo, softening the scene. The netting hangs from rings looped over the gazebo's ceiling hook.

outdoor dining

left: A gazebo furnished with a dining table and chairs allows for savoring meals beneath the stars or for enjoying coffee while reading the morning newspaper. The table also offers a sturdy surface for playing board games, doing homework, or munching an after-school snack. Select accessories that complement the gazebo's style or material if you like. In this case, wrought iron shapes the theme in furniture and candlestands as well as the overall structure.

gazebo rooms

the view from here

The word *gazebo* comes from blending the words *gaze* and *about*. In the garden, a gazebo is not only a strong focal point; it also commands a vantage point. Position your gazebo to survey delightful scenery, such as a water feature, a planting bed, or a panoramic vista. Design your gazebo with the view in mind, elevating the floor to enhance a vantage point.

Consider the approach to your gazebo as well. If it's in the midst of an expanse of lawn, no path may be necessary. But if it's tucked among plantings, install a walkway. Choose path materials that complement the gazebo's style and surrounding plantings. Use decking to connect a gazebo to a patio or to your house.

easy transition

above right: This gazebo extends over the edge of a pond and uses concrete piers for support and decking for flooring. Simple furnishings, including a hammock chair and canvas deck chairs, suit the retreat's casual theme. The design works as a transition into the landscape.

capture attention

right: A gazebo can serve as a focal point, even in a small yard. This backyard boasted an eye-grabbing feature: a hill. The addition of this elegantly contoured gazebo embellished an attractive scene. Citrus trees adorn the slope and provide a solid green backdrop to the gazebo, while a profusion of roses and perennials envelop the structure with color.

modern art

left: **A nontraditional gazebo design aims for a playful or flamboyant effect, rather than matching the house. A table and chairs tucked inside the hideaway provide a refreshing perch for viewing the surrounding wildflowers. The gazebo's height draws eyes through the meadow planting, forming an effective focal point. Slatted sides cast ample shade for garden visitors.**

tepees

native heritage

In today's garden, a tepee offers a simple but effective structure, providing height in otherwise flat planting schemes and forming a shelter that's affordable and easy to build. Tepees work well in children's gardens, creating small spaces for big imaginations to weave adventures.

To construct a retreat replete with adventure and fun, start with 6- to 8-foot poles, such as metal reinforcing rods, saplings, or bamboo. Lash the poles together at least 6 inches from their top ends, and then spread the free ends away from one another, creating a circular shape. Position the poles to form a distinct entrance. Anchor your

powwow playhouse

below: Branches form a tepee that's too pretty to cover with vines. Stock the tepee with child-size chairs, and it will certainly provide allure.

structure to the ground by pushing the poles 6 to 12 inches into the soil. Use hollow-style post anchors to secure the saplings in place. Have children plant pole beans near the base of each support. Teach kids how to tell when beans are ripe, and you'll have them eating their vegetables in no time.

tip-top tepee

left: Design a vine-entwined dining room courtesy of a metal reinforcing rod tepee and easy-to-grow morning glories. Each of the four 10-foot-tall rods rises from the corner of a plank-enclosed mulch floor. The tops of the rods are lashed securely with wire and topped with a metal fencepost finial. A classic bistro-style table and chairs fit neatly inside the tepee.

living rooms

family central

This house-hugging addition transformed a steep, unused backyard into a family-focused room with all the perks of a luxury vacation. A sunny area for dining and barbecuing occupies one end of the deck, a vine-smothered arbor beckons with cooling shade at the other end, and a sunken hot tub bubbles in between. The three areas add up to an outdoor family room and entertainment center that has become the heart of the home.

Redwood decking and white railings create a clean look that

classical tradition

right: **The classic design of deck-railing details complements the traditional-style house. The deck's middle section drops down to an inviting spa area. Lower railings near the spa permit an unhindered view from inside the kitchen.**

complements the house. Marble-composite columns hold the arbor aloft with architectural finesse and promise a longer life than wood. Barefoot-friendly redwood resists cracking; it doesn't require headed nails, which cause hot spots. Easy-to-clean white resin furniture and cushions offer casual elegance for entertaining.

The spa offers year-round enjoyment. A peaked arbor over the main deck room features a dense cover of vines and a ceiling fan. A 48-inch square of glass ceiling fits into the arbor's peak and protects the fan from above. A ceiling fan lowers the temperature in the vine-canopied room 8 to 10 degrees.

family-friendly features

- Build multiple levels. Give kids their own play area, such as a sandbox or patio adjacent to a deck.

- Include a toy-storage area for the kids to store their stuff. Tuck a storage shed for large toys under the deck.

- Plan for safety. Top the spa with a lockable safety cover. Don't allow the spa's water temperature to exceed 104 degrees F.

- Opt for wide steps. Two-foot-wide stairs prove toddler negotiable and provide extra seating. They also offer room for pots of herbs.

natural cooling

left: **A double-top arbor boasts cool shade in the living room beneath it and easy care. The unfinished top layer of the ceiling supports wisteria and trumpet vines. The lower structure holds a ceiling fan.**

living rooms

easy livin' room

When you're ready to turn your dreams of an outdoor living room into reality, keep your plans focused and make the space meet your needs. An inviting retreat (*right* and *opposite*) replaces an old, overgrown backyard with finesse. A corner pavilion with a dining nook, a fire pit, and a cozy sitting area make the confines of a 30×30-foot area seem expansive.

When designing your outdoor living room, position patios, decks, and walkways first. Create different levels for interest and depth. Splurge on features that pay off in the long run, such as adding electricity, water, and computer hookup to the area.

corner on luxury

right: With its skylights, ceiling fan, futons, and privacy fence, this corner pavilion makes a comfortable room for resting or entertaining. The lattice inserts overhead permit airflow into the space.

spatially challenged

above: Narrow spaces plague many American yards, but they become outdoor hideaways with a little space-enhancing sleight of hand. A privacy fence packs powerful magic. Its lattice windows foster a feeling of openness, while wall-clinging planters and lighting maximize space. Small-scale furniture from a secondhand store takes on new life with paint and cushions.

dining rooms

pavilion pleasures

In many cases, the first room that sprouts in the
garden is a dining room. A dining area needs no
more than a table and chairs to dress the space
in simple or elegant style. If you entertain often
or want to enjoy alfresco meals on a regular basis,
consider adding an overhead structure, walls, or
flooring to set the room apart. Of course, it's easiest
to set up a dining area on an existing deck or a
patio. A pergola or an overhanging tree provides
ample covering to create a sense of place. For the
serious entertainer, a dining pavilion (*right* and
below) may be in order.

This 8×20-foot latticework wonder offers
a sheltered, comfortable place for a dozen or
more friends to gather and linger over food
and conversation. A generous table and a mix
of folding chairs easily fit the space. Draped folds

natural air-conditioning

below: **Various openings in the lath structure
contribute to circulation through this fresh-air
dining room. The design features include large
stair-step-cutout doorways in the pavilion's
front, windows in the back that swing open
or latch shut, and 8-foot-wide open ends.**

of weatherproof fabric provide softness and privacy, evoking visions of Tuscany or Provence. Soft electric lighting gently brightens the nighttime scene.

Construct your pavilion with weather-worthy materials. Plastic lath walls create privacy, permit air movement, and conjure an illusion of spaciousness in the narrow area. Underfoot, vinyl plank flooring provides a surface that's sturdy and carefree.

The matching pedestals outside the structure continue the formal design with plastic lath that never needs painting. The urn-topped pedestals extend the pavilion's welcoming aura. Foliage tapestries skirt the doorways with the jewel tones of coleus, plectranthus, and sweet potato vine.

have a seat

Outdoor dining lends itself to lingering for hours, so cater to comfort in your seating.

- Add cushions covered in weather-resistant fabrics to soften hard seats.

- Choose lightweight pieces, such as plastic or canvas chairs, for easy mobility.

- Mix and match styles, choosing chairs in either the same color scheme or made from the same materials.

- Consider storage options. Folding chairs take up a minimum of storage space. Stackable resin seats also store easily.

common thread

left: **Plastic lath weaves a unifying architectural theme throughout this garden, from pedestals and dining room walls to garden tool storage, fencing, screens, and accents. The white lath suits the formal look, whereas a wood tone would appear more rustic.**

dining rooms

set the mood

Mealtime takes on a new dimension when it's accompanied by birdsong or a starry night. Simple touches in your outdoor dining room are sure to heighten the festive mood and make conversation sparkle and the food taste better.

Load a welcoming side table with beverages, a variety of glasses, a corkscrew, plenty of ice, and cocktail napkins. Arrange chairs, benches, and small tables in comfortable groupings to encourage mingling.

Set a table that's garden-fresh looking and inviting. A centerpiece of flowers adds instant charm. Make either a low arrangement or one of extra-long stems in a tall vase that won't interfere with conversing. Float individual blooms in glass bowls for place setting pizzazz. Or sprinkle flower petals

aegean style

above: Host a Mediterranean-style dinner by using white linens, pots full of bright red geraniums, lots of fresh fruit and cheese, and flickering lantern light.

buffet bench

right: Press traditional garden gear into fancifully functional dining roles. Use a potting bench as a stylish buffet or use a wheelbarrow as an ice chest.

on the table just before guests arrive. Gather sprigs of fresh herbs into small bouquets tied with raffia; set a bouquet at each place setting as a fragrant party favor.

Extend the garden theme with lightweight, terra-cotta-look containers as serving pieces for ice, bottled drinks, salad, bread, and such. Available in a variety of sizes, shapes, and styles, the classy-looking styrene pots come without drainage holes and won't chip, crack, or break.

Light the night with candles, twinkle lights strung through trees and shrubs, and lanterns. Include relaxing sounds in your outdoor decor scheme, such as a trickling fountain or soft music.

simple decor

left: **Cushioned chairs, a fabric-covered table, and a sisal rug help turn an old shed into a cozy room for coffee or tea. A vintage chandelier makes a perfect candelabra.**

garden rooms | **149**

kitchen garden rooms

homegrown haven

Who says vegetable gardens must hide in the backyard and be sprawling or unattractive? Turn your vegetable patch into a garden room and it will be a source of pride and pleasure. Kitchen gardens originally earned their keep in colonial America, providing fare for everyday meals and colorful flowers for everyone's delight.

Practicality still reigns in kitchen gardens, where typically formal overall designs feature tidy plantings and efficient structures. Tepees, arbors, or fences provide vertical growing space for tall or vining crops. Vegetables grow alongside herbs, fruits, and flowers in

formal finery

right: **The handsome design of a kitchen garden combines neat raised beds with gravel paths and eye-catching focal points. Situated near the house, the produce proves most handy to the kitchen.**

attractive tapestries of colors and textures.

Begin your kitchen garden design by laying out beds and paths in a sunny location. Raised beds offer accessibility and excellent drainage. Plan and plant an ornamental, productive garden room, including spring greens, summer fruits, and annual flowers, plus herbs and root crops. Depending on the size of the area, carve out space for strolling or sitting. A bistro-style table and chairs, a bench, and rocking chairs are options. Or hang a hammock for a place to dream about the next season's crops.

roundtable garden
above left: **A hub-and-spoke-style garden includes roomy paths for ample access. Beds less than 5 feet wide make tending effortless from any direction. Trellis walls support vining crops.**

growing up
left: **Trellises and arbors enable tomatoes, squash, and dipper gourds to grow in a sunny spot.**

garden rooms | **151**

sleeping rooms

dream on

Before air-conditioning, people commonly slept outdoors and on sleeping porches to beat the heat of summer nights. Not what you would ordinarily think of as a garden bed, an outdoor sleeping room offers a place to sleep, read, or daydream. It's a restful place with a view of the garden, with or without walls or windows.

Begin by choosing an area with cover overhead: Create an under-the-eaves refuge or tuck a bunk under a balcony. Set up a traditional sleeping room in a porch or sunroom. Turn a deck or a patio into a bedroom with a canopy and curtains.

Have the joys of sleeping under the stars with all the comforts of home. Where bedding is exposed to the elements, select materials with weatherability in mind. Camping pads, an air mattress, canvas cots, and hammocks have great weather-resistant traits. If you prefer, use a waterproof plastic liner to cover a mattress on a platform. Drape mosquito netting or sheer fabric around the bed or the room for an elegant insect barrier. Hang light-dimming roller shades.

Pile on comfort with soft bedding, including plenty of washable pillows and amenities, such as a ceiling fan, a rocking chair, a table stocked with books, and an adequate reading light. Include a nightstand to hold a glass of water or a cup of tea, but no alarm clock. Let the sun and the birds provide a wake-up call.

sleeping quarters

right: Vine-clad trellises and columns help sequester the sleeping room. Nearby plantings bolster privacy and sweetly fragrant dreams. The scent of roses and jasmine waft through the air.

bedtime stories

above: Position a room for resting on the most private side of your home. This peaceful portico, enveloped by fragrant plantings and painted to resemble a tropical sea, evokes a delightful South Pacific atmosphere. The bed mimics a *hikeee* (hee-key-eh-ya, a large Hawaiian couch) and proves irresistible as a place for reading or napping.

scents to nap by

Fragrant flowers allure with their perfume; some scents promote relaxation and rest.

chamomile	lavender
freesia	lilac
gardenia	lily
honeysuckle	rose
hyacinth	stock
jasmine	tuberose

sleeping rooms

sweet dreams

Once a part of life on sultry summer nights, especially in the South, the sleeping porch offers a dreamy setting where the music of nature lulls you to sleep and nudges you awake.

A screened porch begs to be enjoyed, with its breeze-friendly walls and sometimes-shady, sometimes-sunny scenery. If your home doesn't include a porch, you have options. Settle a comfortable old sofa on a covered patio or hang a hammock under a balcony. Wherever a roof and a wall meet, there's potential for a sleeping room.

outdoor ease

right: Creature comforts complete a room designed for rest. Drape a sofa with a matelassé spread, a snuggly throw, and big pillows—naptime awaits.

Select furniture that caters to relaxation and rest. Choose a bed based on its functionality and your budget. A daybed, for instance, doubles as seating. Cart a lightweight futon outdoors to make a chaise for two. Recycle a hideabed that's perfectly comfortable but benefits from a slipcover.

Nothing says take a break better than a hammock, whether it's dangling from a ceiling or perched in an iron stand. Suspend your hammock in a spot with plenty of swinging room. To hang a hammock, choose heavy-duty eyebolts and chain; screw hooks securely into ceiling joists, posts, or wall studs.

breezy bed

below: **Adopt tropical-isle style to create a room that's big on comfort, color, and seaside charm. Choose a scheme that relies on this trio of materials to make decorating a snap: canvas, rattan, and wicker.**

meditation rooms

peaceful escape

In a world of haste and hassle, your garden offers a place to unwind, find peace of mind, and restore your sensibilities. Tend your garden as a sanctuary for your soul and it will provide you with a place to sit back, relax, breathe deeply, rest, and rejuvenate.

While gardening encourages healthy exercise and provides plenty of fresh air and sunshine, connecting with nature calms the mind. Just as a garden represents a spiritual haven for many, you can create a refuge in your yard to suit your vision of paradise. Call it your yoga garden, the reading room, your pondering place, or whatever. A garden sanctuary includes basic elements, whether you desire seclusion, quiet, solitude, or a place to sit and watch the birds.

Begin by closing your eyes and imagining yourself in this restful place. Then find a spot for

a place for repose

Every garden contains the building blocks of a meditative escape.

- **conceal and heal:** Partially enclose an existing seating area to foster solitude. Silence soothes the soul.

- **putter and ponder:** Find refreshment in basic gardening activities. Let weeding, digging, and planting relax your mind.

- **rest and refuel:** A rocking chair, a swing, or a hammock has soothing appeal.

- **naturalize and nurture:** Commune with nature's beauty and peace via simple building materials: stone, wood, bamboo, and clay.

take a break
right: A garden that fosters relaxation and serenity includes a sheltered place to sit. From here, you can look out and see what's beautiful about your garden (instead of focusing on what needs to be done).

your garden escape: under a tree or tucked into a secluded corner; a place protected from wind that captures sunshine in winter and shade in summer. Choose shrubs or a structure to shape a secluded room, hidden from view of the house and from nearby traffic.

What do you need to relax? Soft plants, fragrant herbs, and pastel blooms cater to the senses. Do you prefer tinkling bells, a wind chime, a creaking windmill, or silence? Would a water feature rest your mind? Consider adding a lily pond or a still, shallow pool that inspires reflection.

year-round retreat
left: An enclosed meditation room sits in a quiet corner of the garden, offering a delightful haven for contemplation. The folding doors open wide enough to blur the line between the room and outside.

meditation rooms

worlds apart

Find sanctuary in your garden by designing a room that will rejuvenate and refresh you. Any garden can become a peaceful haven when furnishings include the following:

an inviting entry:

Use an arbor, an arch, or a gate to mark the threshold to your special place. Create a welcoming ambience with a climbing rose, a sign, or a bell.

comfortable seating: A bench, a reclining chaise, or a bed invites you to stretch out or put up your feet. A cushioned

viewing platform

right: Reed matting from a home improvement store, bamboo poles, and a beach-combed dock panel outfit a room for garden contemplation. Embroidered pillows and a cotton throw soften the seating. Mosquito netting comes in handy too.

seat with a backrest proves restful. Plant a soft, mossy rug to lie upon.

low maintenance: Set up plantings, including those in containers, with a regular supply of water from drip irrigation automated with a timer. Construct a handy place to store cushions, candles, and other accessories for your haven.

restful oasis

left: Still or moving, water brings a reflective element to any garden. A few floating blooms in a lotus bowl, believed by Hindus to inspire tranquillity and help purify the spirit, reflect nature's beauty and peace.

artful inspiration

left: A patterned pebble mosaic engages the mind in thoughtful reverie. Gather stones at a quarry or rock yard. Sort stones by size, shape, and color. Practice laying stones in patterns on a flat surface. Frame the design with edging. Set stones at ground level in 1 inch of mortar on a 2-inch base of sand and crushed rock. Work quickly and in small sections because mortar sets within minutes.

bathing rooms

shower power

An outdoor shower or bath proves cool, convenient, and decadently refreshing as it washes away the effects of toiling in the garden. Site a shower in a private alcove behind shrubbery or walls. This bathing room *(right)* sequesters a shower with recycled boards. Salvaged cupboards, a stone floor, and secondhand furnishings complete the room. The rustic ambience enhances the delight of bathing beneath the sun or moon. Cover a shower with rafters and plant vines to cloak them, if the stall is visible from above.

shower amenities

right: Burlap curtains add privacy; a cupboard keeps soap, shampoo, and towels handy. A potted gardenia scents the air.

left: Locate a shower in a sunny place and enjoy the sun's warmth when you bathe. Either construct the enclosure or install a prefabricated unit. Incorporate nonslip flooring of wood decking or flagstone. Interplant stones or pavers with creeping mint or thyme.

let it pour

You'll be set to get wet when you add a shower to your garden.

- Construct an enclosure on the side of an existing building, such as a garage, a potting shed, or a storage building. Guarantee privacy with sidewalls and a door or dense shrubbery.

- Build waterproof walls of vinyl planking or lattice. If you prefer wood, choose rot-resistant lumber, such as cedar. Seal wood with a water-repellant preservative.

- In cold-winter regions, include a valve to permit draining the plumbing and turning off the water supply (to prevent rupturing frozen pipes) in late fall.

- A portable camp shower is a snap to install. Look for solar-heated models to ensure warm water.

bathing rooms

bathroom decor

Imagine soaking in a warm, bubbly tub in shimmery sunshine or under sparkly stars. As a place for luxury and pleasure, the bathing garden is an ancient concept with recently renewed appeal. A bath soothes the mind as well as the muscles.

Create an outdoor bathing room with a tub for soaking. Save a claw-footed tub from a remodeling project or acquire one at a salvage store. Fill the bath using a bucket or a hose; let cool water sit in the sun until it's warm enough for a bath. Or have a plumber connect your outdoor tub or shower to indoor hot water. Warm water soothes; cool water exhilarates.

Furnish your bathing room with convenience, comfort, and pleasure in mind. A plant stand forms a handy towel rack. A small table or stool holds a refreshing drink for sipping while bathing. Fill a basket full of your favorite bathtime necessities: soap, essential oils, a loofah sponge, scented candles, a favorite book or magazine, and thick towels.

earthly delights

Grow a garden that's ripe with plants renowned as boons to bathing. Gather leaves or blossoms, fresh or dried, into a muslin or cheesecloth bag. Tie the bag closed with cotton string. Float the bag in bathwater or hang it under the faucet while filling the tub. Float additional leaves or flowers on bathwater.

- **soothing:** lavender, chamomile flowers, lemon balm

- **stimulating:** peppermint, rosemary, spearmint, anise hyssop

- **therapeutic:** sage, rosemary, peppermint, eucalyptus, thyme

- **romantic:** rose petals, calendula petals, jasmine flowers, gardenia flowers

private oasis

left: Soothe the senses with a relaxing outdoor bath tucked into a secluded part of your garden, sheltered by shrubs or other tall plants or enclosed by walls. Build a screen of lattice, bamboo, reed, or fabric for more privacy. Train vines on trellises to make living curtains; choose fragrant flowering plants, such as jasmine or climbing rose.

bathing rooms

relaxation oasis

A hot, bubbling spa suits an outdoor room made for unwinding. Design your soaking sanctuary to be cloistered and colorful. Cultivate privacy with a fence, a hedge, or lattice screens. If the spa is visible from above, provide overhead cover with a pergola or trees. Enrich the scene with colorful and fragrant plants.

Test spas by soaking in them at local retail outlets. It's the only way to know how the seats and jets feel. Install a nonslip decking material around your spa, and lock a cover over the water when the spa is not in use.

seating options

right: Include seating outside your spa for those taking a break from the warm water or those not inclined to get wet. Choose water-repellant cushions.

decked out

left: Build an elevated deck area around an above-ground spa to create the look of a sunken pool. Encircle the deck with bushy perennials to enhance the feeling of a meadow retreat.

cool pool

below: For a small backyard, design an in-ground spa that's square or rectangular to suggest the feel of a pool. Landscape with plants that won't shed leaves into the spa, such as palms, scheffleras, or pines.

garden rooms | **165**

potting rooms

garden sheds

The ideal shed, whether fancy and furnished to the hilt or simple and strictly functional, contains a gardener's tools, togs, soil amendments, and pots. A shed stores and organizes garden gear in a location not too far from garden paths.

Situate a shed to be a focal point in your garden if you like. Design it with details that meld good looks and utility. Build windows, for instance, and then add window boxes for a fanciful touch. Surround the shed with a porch that's wide enough to hold a pile of firewood as well as chairs and a table.

Soften the structure with climbing roses,

double-duty shed

right: A 15×12-foot garden house boasts multiple personalities. During the day, this shed passes muster as a work space and utility building; after dusk, it segues into an entertaining mode as a serving center.

clematis, or annual vines. Carve pathways that wander through your garden to the shed, making the journey as delightful as the destination.

Focus on function when furnishing the shed. If you plan to arrange bouquets of garden flowers there, rig a supply of running water. Add electrical outlets and lighting. Stock potting soil and birdseed in moisture- and critter-proof containers. Select a flooring material that's easy to sweep clean. Build doors wide enough to accommodate a wheelbarrow or a garden cart.

fresh-air flair
left: **Latticework walls and an open, peaked roof give the shed an airy feel while containing the necessities for everyday garden chores. The utilitarian structure allows ample space for hanging tools on pegs.**

potting rooms

swanky shed

Supply your outbuilding with modern amenities. Beyond basic plumbing and electricity you may wish to include a computer hookup to transform your shed into an office annex or studio. Run a phone line to it and eliminate mad dashes indoors to catch calls.

Where there's room, furnish a garden house to increase its uses. A refrigerator promises a convenient cold drink, while a wet bar earns its keep at garden parties. Include a dining table and chairs for cozy meals. Set up a desk or a drawing board and a stool; line a wall with a daybed.

open and shut

left: A waist-high counter tops storage shelves inside the potting shed. Drawers corral handtools and flower-arranging supplies. Extra-long drawers accommodate long-legged plant markers and some tools.

plant caddy

below: A galvanized metal box keeps frequently used tools and other essentials neat looking and within easy reach. Ample, additional storage areas help minimize countertop clutter.

potting rooms

garden galley

Construct a garden workroom that's designed to hold gadgets and make gardening easier. Tucked along the outside wall of a garage, this efficient space includes a counter for potting chores with a generous storage area tucked below for pots and soil. A carefully positioned trellis, skirted with abundant plantings, screens the potting room from a nearby patio. Brick pavers form a sturdy floor that matches the adjacent patio. A garden hose, mounted on the end of the bench, trickles on demand. Rarely used, long–handled garden tools hang inside the garage or on the lattice wall.

workroom disguise

right: **A 9×12-foot vine-laced trellis screens the 3-foot-deep potting niche from nearby patio seating. The brick platform in front of the trellis holds a collection of potted plants and hides a plumbing access area.**

hidden asset

above: Outside the back door, this 12-foot-long workbench hosts a variety of tasks, from transplanting seedlings and washing homegrown vegetables to completing carpentry projects. An overhanging ceiling protects the cabinets and countertop from rainfall. Under the counter, half whiskey barrels store soil amendments.

potting rooms

work and play

For many gardeners, space-constrained yards and community landscape codes limit the addition of a full-scale potting shed. A multifunctional garden bench is an answer. Designed as a handsome piece of garden furniture, the unit combines a convenient place for potting with storage. As a serving surface, it makes entertaining easier.

Made from ½-inch plywood, the bench includes a place to inset plastic dishpans, which are perfect for holding soil, water, or drinks on ice. The roomy storage area accommodates pillows, linens, candles, and outdoor tableware.

neat and handy

right: **A well-designed potting bench reduces garden-gadget clutter. Store soil in a plastic garbage can; gather tools and plant labels in a decorative basket. Stack pots on a sliding shelf to enhance their access.**

out of sight

left: Storing outdoor cushions when not in use increases their longevity, but their bulkiness requires ample space. A tall sideboard-style addition to this potting bench protects pillows and similar accessories. Stack lidded plastic bins inside the cupboard to increase storage efficiency.

potting bench inventory

A well-stocked potting bench is a putterer's paradise.

- Place bagged soil and amendments (sand, peat moss, perlite) in covered containers, such as plastic bins or garbage cans.

- Organize hand tools by function and size, using baskets or tall buckets. Separate sharp-bladed tools from digging tools to avoid accidental cuts.

- Run a length of hose from the nearest spigot to your bench; attach a turn-off valve. If you're plumbing from scratch, include a hot-water spigot.

- Gather the goods to sharpen, oil, and clean tools (lubricating oil, wire brush, sharpening stone, screwdrivers, pliers). Store them under cover.

little getaways

garden haven

Everybody needs a private place where they can steal away for a while. A little getaway zone offers a place for solitude and intimacy. Complete with furniture, you can curl up and drift away in daydreams to anywhere in the world within a few feet of your back door.

As you plan a garden retreat, think about when you will spend time there and what your activities will include. Will it be a casual, everyday spot for solitary reading and sipping something soothing or a place for

cabana corner

right: Lay a small brick patio in the middle of a perennial bed. A colorful canvas chair, a table, and the fragrance of lavender combine to create a restful spot in the garden. The folding furnishings transport easily, set up quickly, and conserve storage space.

weekend entertaining? Do you want to make room for kids and pets, or do you hope to hide from household hubbub? Do you plan to dine as you watch the sunset or do you desire a lunch spot that affords cool respite from midday heat? List your priorities, then narrow your choices.

Perhaps your yard includes an area with an innate quality that sets it apart from the surroundings. For example, place your hideaway in a sunken area, a sunny place, or a naturally enclosed spot. When accessorizing, keep furniture and other pieces simple and suitable for the ambience you're seeking.

towers of flowers

below: **This streetside retreat transports a gardener to a world filled with tall, flowering perennials. The sitting area, hidden within feet of the house, lurks at the end of the path.**

garden rooms | **175**

little getaways

under cover

A getaway zone doesn't
require space that's set
apart from the rest of
your home and garden.
When it takes root in
the midst of everything,
the place is bound to
get frequent use.

Define your getaway
with walls and flooring.
A wall may shout
or hint of a room's
existence, depending
on whether the wall is
towering or ankle-high.
A change in surface
underfoot marks a
clear transition from
one space to another.
A distinct floor strategy
magnifies the air of
separateness, especially
in a room that lacks
tall walls.

tuck-under retreat

right: This little
getaway is capped
by a balcony and is
an extension of the
house, providing a
sense of continuity
between indoors
and outdoors.

petite palace

left: You don't need wide-open space to incorporate a stately gazebo. This scaled-down structure outfits a small side yard with larger-than-life style, featuring clean design lines and built-in benches.

nifty nook

below left: Knee-high hedges form understated walls that partially enclose a circular nook. Clearcut boundaries of the room include a lattice-panel backdrop and a flagstone floor that picks up where adjacent lawn leaves off. Nearby trees provide cooling shade.

a room of your own

When planning a little getaway, include these features to ensure your satisfaction.

- Enclose at least three sides of the room to create a sense of seclusion, using hedges, walls, or tightly woven lattice.

- Define entrances. Add a door or gate that you can pull shut to enhance a sequestered feeling.

- Provide seating for one or two that commands a view.

- Include special plants, such as fragrant herbs, that greet you with their refreshing scents or containers packed with a variety of annuals in your favorite colors.

little getaways

sanctuary seating

Any secluded spot
promises getaway
potential. Once you
select the space, fill it
with furniture that's
stylish, comfortable,
and easy-care. The
garden seat itself, like
the tended loveliness
that surrounds it,
should be a haven, an
art form, a reflection of
your needs and tastes.

If you want to
stretch out, include
a chaise lounge or
hang a hammock.
When comfort is the
goal, plant a cushioned
Adirondack chair for a
place to sit back,
unwind, and drink in
the scenery. Every good
project starts with good
planning. For other
types of getaways,
search through our
home plans at
**www.bhg.com/
bkhouseplans**

fanciful furnishings

right: Furnish your
little getaway with a
whimsical focal point,
such as a topiary
chair made with PVC
pipe, chicken wire,
and sphagnum moss.
Embroider the seat
cover with ivy.

hide and seek

above: The allure of the best garden retreats comes from their privacy, as well as the ongoing seasonal appeal of the surroundings. Choose a hideaway with that in mind. When the backdrop brims with natural beauty, furnish your secret place as simply as possible.

swinging shelter

left: A covered glider rocks to the beat of good conversation in a swing designed for kids of all ages. Set a comparable structure beneath a canopy of trees or at the end of a path. Purchase a ready-made glider or build one from scratch.

resources

arbors, trellises, & structures
Arboria
LWO Corp.
P.O. Box 17125
Portland, OR 97217
503/286-5372
www.arboria.com

Archadeck U.S. Structures, Inc.
2112 W. Laburnum Ave., Suite 100
Richmond, VA 23227
800/722-4668
www.archadeck.com

Bloomsbury Market
403 South Cedar Lake Rd.
Bryn Mawr, MN 55405
800/999-2411
www.bloomsburymkt.com

art for the garden
Ancient Graffiti
52 Seymour St.
Middlebury, VT 05753
888/725-6632
www.ancientgraffiti.com

Garden Smiles; George Carruth
211 Mechanic St.
Waterville, OH 43566
419/878-5412
www.carruthstudio.com

Sunspots Studio
202 S. Lewis St.
Staunton, VA 24401
540/885-8557
www.sunspots.com

birdhouses
Heartwood, Architecture for the Birds
P.O. Box 298
Star, MS 39167
601/845-6530
www.heartwood-online.com

concrete stain
H & C Concrete Products
The Sherwin-Williams Co.
101 Prospect Ave. NW
Cleveland, OH 44115
800/474-3794
www.sherwin-williams.com

containers
Frontgate
5566 West Chester Rd.
West Chester, OH 45069
800/626-6488
www.frontgate.com

Stonesmith Garden Vessels
P.O. Box 713
Cambria, CA 93428
805/927-3707
www.stonesmith.com

Tierra International
P.O. Box 710
Jasper, IN 47547-0710
888/812-3384
www.tierraint.com

everything garden
Smith & Hawken
P.O. Box 431
Milwaukee, WI 53201-0431
800/940-1170
www.smithandhawken.com

Gardener's Supply Co.
128 Intervale Rd.
Burlington, VT 05401
888/833-1412
www.gardeners.com

fabrics & cushions (for outdoor use)
Outdoor Fabrics
P.O. Box 160466
Miami, FL 33116
800/640-3559
www.outdoorfabrics.com

Plow & Hearth
P.O. Box 6000
Madison, VA 22727-1600
800/627-1712
www.plowhearth.com

fencing
Hoover Fence Co.
P.O. Box 563
Newton Falls, OH 44444
330/358-2335
www.hooverfence.net

Lyric Japanese Antiques
8705 15th Ave N.W.
Seattle, WA 98117
206/782-4062
www.lyricjapanese.com

Mid-Atlantic Vinyl Products
P.O. Box 41985
Fredericksburg, VA 22404
800/978-4695
www.mvp97.com

Walpole Woodworkers, Inc.
767 East St.
Walpole, MA 02081
800/343-6948
www.walpolewoodworkers.com

fire pits & patio fireplaces
Exterior Accents
9931-B Rose Commons Dr.
Huntersville, NC 28078
888/551-5211
www.exterior-accents.com

Final Touches
115 Morris St., P.O. Box 2557
Blowing Rock, NC 28605
877/506-2741
www.finaltouches.com

Fire Science, Inc.
8350 Main St.
Williamsville, NY 14221
716/633-1130
www.fire-science.com

fountains
Beckett Corp.
5931 Campus Circle Dr.
Irving, TX 75063
888/232-5388
www.888beckett.com

Stone Forest
P.O. Box 2840
Santa Fe, NM 87504
888/682-2987
www.stoneforest.com

fruit trees for espalier
Miller Nurseries
5060 West Lake Rd.
Canandaigua, NY 14424-8904
800/836-9630
www.millernurseries.com

Stark Bros.
P.O. Box 10
Louisiana, MO 63353
800/325-4180
www.starkbros.com

furniture

Gloster Furniture, Inc.
606 Broad St. P.O. Box 738
South Boston, VA 24592
888/456-7837
www.gloster.com

Tidewater Workshop
1515 Grant St.
Egg Harbor, NJ 08215
800/666-8433
www.tidewaterworkshop.com

Tropitone Furniture Co.
5 Marconi
Irvine, CA 92618
949/951-2010
www.tropitone.com

garden design stencil & landscape design notebook

Lee Valley Tools
P.O. Box 1780
Ogdensburg, NY 13669-6780
800/871-8158
www.leevalleytools.com

gazebos

Gazebo Junction, Inc.
2627 Kaneville Ct.
Geneva, IL 60134
800/966-9261
www.gazebojunction.com

Vixen Hill Manufacturing Co.
Main St.
Elverson, PA 19520
800/423-2766
www.vixenhill.com

greenhouses

Santa Barbara Greenhouses
721 Richmond Ave.
Oxnard, CA 93030
800/544-5276
www.sbgreenhouse.com

Sundance Supply
P.O. Box 225
Olga, WA 98279
800/776-2534
www.sundancesupply.com

hammocks and swings

101 Hamocks
512/233-6524
www.101hammocks.com

Chairs of the Sky and Air
3525 Del Mar Heights
San Diego, CA 92130
800/488-2756
www.chairsoftheskyandair.com

Golden Hammocks
2220 Division St.
Waite Park, MN 56387
320/685-7653
www.goldenhammocks.com

Nags Head Hammocks
Milepost 9 Hwy. 158
Nags Head, NC 27959
800/344-6433
www.nagshead.com

Sky Chairs
828 Pearl St.
Boulder, CO 80302
800/759-8759
www.skychairs.com

outdoor lighting

Armadilla Wax Works, Inc.
2651 N. Industrial Way
Prescott Valley, AZ 86314
800/247-6045
www.waccents.com

Intermatic, Inc.
Intermatic Plaza
Spring Grove, IL 60081-9698
815/675-7000
www.intermatic.com

Lorijane Studio
118 B S. Acacia Ave.
Solana Beach, CA 92075
info@lorijane.com
www.lorijane.com

mosquito netting

Barre Army/Navy Store
955 N. Main St.
Barre, VT 05641
800/448-7965
www.vtarmynavy.com/bugstuff.htm

motorized awnings

General Awning & Fabric
160-6660 Greybar Rd.
Richmond, BC Canada V6W 1H9
888/693-8833
www.generalawning.com

Betterliving Patio Rooms
926 Highway 72 E
Athens, AL 35611
800/977-4151
www.blpatiorooms.com

outdoor showers

Comfort House
189-V Frelinghuysen Ave.
Newark, NJ 07114-1595
800/359-7701
www.comforthouse.com

Specialty Pool Products, Inc.
110 Main St.
Broad Brook, CT 06016-0388
800/983-7665
www.poolproducts.com

recycled materials

QuickBrick
U.S. Rubber Recycling, Inc.
2225 Via Cerro, Unit B
Riverside, CA 92509
888/473-8453
www.usrubber.com

ENVIROFORM Recycled Products, Inc.
28 Seeley Rd.
Geneva, NY 14456
800/789-1819
www.enviroform.com

reed and bamboo matting

Bamboo Hardwoods
6402 Roosevelt Way NE
Seattle, WA 98115-6619
206/529-0978
www.bamboohardwoods.com

Cane & Basket Supply Co.
1283 South Cochran Ave.
Los Angeles, CA 90019
323/939-9644
www.canebasket.com

Conneticut Cane and Reed Co.
Box 762
Manchester, CT 06045
800/227-8498
www.caneandreed.com

index

index

index

index

index

index

photo credits

Chris Jacobson
GARDENART
152, 153
Walpole Woodworkers
161

metric conversions

u.s. units to metric equivalents

to convert from	multiply by	to get
Inches	25.400	Millimeters
Inches	2.540	Centimeters
Feet	30.480	Centimeters
Feet	0.3048	Meters
Yards	0.9144	Meters
Square inches	6.4516	Square centimeters
Square feet	0.0929	Square meters
Square yards	0.8361	Square meters
Acres	0.4047	Hectares
Cubic inches	16.387	Cubic centimeters
Cubic feet	0.0283	Cubic meters
Cubic feet	28.316	Liters
Cubic yards	0.7646	Cubic meters
Cubic yards	764.550	Liters

metric units to u.s. equivalents

to convert from	multiply by	to get
Millimeters	0.0394	Inches
Centimeters	0.3937	Inches
Centimeters	0.0328	Feet
Meters	3.2808	Feet
Meters	1.0936	Yards
Square centimeters	0.1550	Square inches
Square meters	10.764	Square feet
Square meters	1.1960	Square yards
Hectares	2.4711	Acres
Cubic centimeters	0.0610	Cubic inches
Cubic meters	35.315	Cubic feet
Liters	0.0353	Cubic feet
Cubic meters	1.308	Cubic yards
Liters	0.0013	Cubic yards

To convert from degrees Celsius (C) to degrees Fahrenheit (F), multiply by $\frac{9}{5}$, then add 32.

To convert from degrees Fahrenheit (F) to degrees Celsius (C), first subtract 32, then multiply by $\frac{5}{9}$.